# A LAY MINISTRY BEHIND BARS

# THE
# PRISON
# CONNECTION

## PAUL D. SCHOONMAKER

Judson Press® Valley Forge

THE PRISON CONNECTION

Copyright © 1978
Judson Press, Valley Forge, PA 19481

Unless otherwise indicated, Bible quotations in this volume are in accordance with the Revised Standard Version of the Bible, copyrighted 1952 and 1971 by the Division of Christian Education of the National Council of the Churches of Christ in the United States of America, and are used by permission.

Other versions of the Bible quoted in this book are:

Today's English Version, the *Good News Bible*—Old Testament: Copyright © American Bible Society 1976; New Testament: Copyright © American Bible Society 1966, 1971, 1976. Used by permission. (TEV)

*The Living Bible* (TLB). Copyright 1971 by Tyndale House Publishers, Wheaton, Illinois. Used by permission.

*The Holy Bible,* King James Version. (KJV)

**Library of Congress Cataloging in Publication Data**

Schoonmaker, Paul D.
  The prison connection.

  Includes bibliographical references.
  1. Church work with prisoners—Pennsylvania—
Graterford. 2. Royersford Baptist Church. I. Title.
BV4465.S36    253.7'5    77-17158
ISBN 0-8170-0775-X

# CONTENTS

# ACKNOWLEDGMENTS

Anything that happens in a church that is alive is always the result of many lives interacting with the Spirit of God, never the pastor's work alone. This is the story of many persons who, by the guidance of God, came to experience the "Prison Connection." I mention here those who were pioneers in this ministry: Phyllis and Jim Cunningham, Art and Joan Reppert, George and Julie Williams, Lloyd and David James, Lisa Jespersen, and Ray Beaver.

Some of the material in this book was originally gathered for a doctoral dissertation that I wrote for the San Francisco Theological Seminary. That and the manuscript for this book were written with the guidance of Dr. J. Lynn Leavenworth who not only gave helpful advice but also became personally involved in this ministry.

I want to acknowledge also the help of Janet Mills and Virginia Dearolf, who sympathetically and patiently helped with many retypings, and Genevieve Forsberg, who handled a large volume of correspondence so efficiently.

Finally, I feel a great debt to the Royersford Baptist Church, which was and is such a supportive congregation, and to my wife, Joan, who always knew just what to say when I was tempted to give up on the effort of putting this experience into words.

# The Way It Is

Chuck Davis[1] is on a sidewalk for the first time in three years. As he walks among strangers in Center City Philadelphia, he begins to feel the first signs of panic in the pit of his stomach. Philadelphia is strange territory for a boy who grew up on a farm in Delaware, but Chuck's anxiety does not come from just being in an unfamiliar place. Chuck is afraid because this is his first furlough weekend from prison in preparation for parole, and he does not know how to get back to the home of his weekend host. With good intentions his host had left him off a few hours earlier assuming that Chuck wanted to "see the sights."

But Chuck is not a tourist; he is a lonely man seeking a friendly face. He pulls out a crumpled piece of paper with his host's address and telephone number on it. No one answers the phone. Chuck has no idea as to how to use public transportation; the markings on the buses and subways mean nothing to him. The same shyness that kept him from telling his host that he really did not want to "see the sights" also keeps him from seeking help from strangers. He has a deadline to meet; he must get back soon.

Chuck remembers the name of a friend in the suburbs and gets her telephone number from the operator. He prays that someone will answer. Fortunately she is at home and tries to calm Chuck's fears. She attempts to direct him to the proper bus, but she, too, is not familiar with city transportation.

Chuck tries to follow her advice. As he sits on the bus, he begins to calm himself and look for familiar landmarks. There are none;

and when the driver calls, "End of the line," he is panic-stricken. Time is running out, and the area is nothing like the affluent neighborhood where his host lives. Instead of returning to Center City to try again, Chuck walks down the street in a daze. As he does, the residents note him carefully for he is a black man in a white neighborhood. His confused manner alarms one woman who calls to her husband, "Joe, tell that man to get out of here." Joe does just that. Chuck's confusion about this whole experience keeps him from using his good intelligence, and, confronted by the man's order to "get out," Chuck runs.

A black man running in a white neighborhood is reason enough for Joe to call the police. Chuck soon hears the sirens. His thoughts are simple, "I am on my first furlough weekend . . . if I mess up, I'll never make parole . . . I must not get caught." Chuck runs off the street between houses and lies down in some bushes. The police have no trouble locating him, for the whole neighborhood has been mobilized, and he is quickly pointed out like a hunted animal. As they get closer, Chuck runs into a house; a woman screams; he runs back out . . . into the arms of the police. He is charged with trespassing, resisting arrest, and assault with a deadly weapon. When Chuck asks, "What deadly weapon?" he is told that he was seen with a gun. Chuck carried the customary Afro comb whose heavy black handle sticking out of his pocket might look like a pistol handle to a frightened person. The gun cannot be found.

Chuck will go on trial. His hopes for parole have been dashed. If he is found guilty, it will be a long time before he sees a furlough again.

That is the way it is for Chuck. That is also the way it is for many others in prison: a way of frustration and hopelessness. We know Chuck's story because the woman he called on the phone is a member of our church. Julie Williams is part of a group that meets regularly with Chuck and other prisoners at the State Correctional Institution at Graterford, Pennsylvania, thirty miles from Philadelphia.

However, this is not the end of Chuck's story. In spite of the fact that Chuck felt that he had let us down, we remained his friends. That relationship, enabled by the love of Christ, has kept Chuck going and brought him to the point where he will receive another furlough with one of our church families. It has been set for Easter weekend. In a very real sense it will be a resurrection from death to life for Chuck.

The chapters that follow trace many such patterns that pass through death to life: a pattern of "try, fail, learn, try again," and, sometimes, "victory." In this process we discovered crucial insights into the Scriptures, prisons, and our systems of justice. We also discovered the importance of counting obedience to Christ more important than the satisfactions of outward success or the approval of society.

Yet, these chapters contain the key to hope for society's future. Only when the men and women in our prisons can experience the love of God will they find a sufficient antidote to the anger and bitterness that make them dangerous to themselves and others—an anger and bitterness experienced by most of them since birth. When there is hope for the prisoner, there will be a better life for us all.

This book is both a narrative of what happened to our church in its prison ministry and a resource manual for other Christians and churches who will seek to be obedient to Jesus' words, "I was in prison and you came to me" (Matthew 25:36).

Our congregation has not learned how to solve the vast problems in our present system of justice nor has it been able to change the society that keeps producing those who will be incarcerated.

However, we did learn, and are learning, a great deal about the Good News of Jesus. This is what we want most to share.

### CHAPTER 1

# The Way It Began

Our "Prison Connection" began with a bid on TV sets. About five years ago the State Correctional Institution at Graterford, Pennsylvania, began allowing prisoners to buy small television sets. When the first sets were let out for bid, Phyllis Cunningham, a member of our church, brought a bid from her husband's appliance store to the prison office. Most people could have conducted this piece of business without further involvement, but not Phyllis. It was her first experience within prison walls, and she began to ask questions: "How many men are here?" "What are conditions like?" "Are churches allowed to visit?"

Even though 1,600 men and those who guard them live and work less than ten miles from our church building, it was not until Phyllis shared her information and concern that we ever gave any thought to a ministry there.

The Women's Missionary Society of our church was not known for "making waves"; yet this was the group that first followed up Phyllis's concern. When they discovered that there were men who had not received any communication from the outside world for years, they talked about planning a Christmas program for the men. They spoke with the chaplain, the Reverend Sidney Barnes, and received permission to bring in our choir to sing Christmas carols in the prison chapel. In addition, they were allowed to bring over three thousand homemade cookies so these men might have a "taste" of Christmas.

The program should have been a flop. The men should have

been unmoved by formal choir anthems and angry over the way the guards distributed the cookies. But somehow they got the message that the thirty people who had come were not performing their annual Christmas "duty" but really were searching for a way to care. We found it natural to step off the chapel platform and mingle with some of the men who remained after the program. While Graterford is a maximum security prison and the men at the program had not been screened, it never occurred to us that we were in any danger. These men had nothing on their minds except to hear a friendly word or to talk with a fellow Christian.

As we came home on our church bus, there was a strong feeling expressed that something ought to done about the hunger for human caring we had discovered in talking with these men. So, a few weeks later, we visited the chaplain and told him how some of our church members had found new support and changed attitudes in the small groups that had been meeting among our fellowship. We believed the informality, honesty, and continuity of this kind of group might be helpful within the prison. We suggested that six or eight of us meet with a like number of prisoners weekly. The prison administration approved this basic idea, and we began to plan. At this point we had no idea where this would eventually lead us.

We knew that we had some basic decisions to make: "What would be our purpose?" "Who would participate?" "How would we select topics for discussion?" To do this planning, two of us from the church met in the chaplain's office with two inmates he selected, Jim and Nelson. They outlined the following needs felt among inmates:

—*The need* to experience normal social contacts with outside groups not only to prepare us for eventual release but also to help us survive as persons in a prison environment.
—*The need* to have someone listen to our frustrations.
—*The need* for someone to take a personal interest in our family problems and to contact our families when possible.
—*The need* for someone to help us with some of our legal problems, not as lawyers, but as friends who may be able to say a good word for us.
—*The need* to find or renew a personal, religious faith.

Those of us from the church shared some of our own needs:

—*Our need* to become informed about prisons and what happens to persons in our system of justice.

—*Our need* to test our conviction that God loves *all* persons and has a plan for each one.

—*Our need* to respond to Scriptures, such as Matthew 25:31-46, KJV (". . . inasmuch as ye have done it unto the least of these, my brethren, ye have done it unto me"), and similar verses that were making us feel increasingly uncomfortable in our church pews on Sunday morning.

Together we wrote out a tentative purpose for our group:

Our purpose is to help each person experience the true meaning of Christian redemption as they become free from old bondages and better able to cope with life in and out of prison. (We felt that the word "redemption" was an especially appropriate word since its root meaning in the Scriptures is "to loose from bondage.")

Our further purpose is to help those in the church to have a greater concern for the imprisoned and to share this concern with the community: a concern that should show itself in actions as well as words.

Finally, our purpose is to bridge the gap between prison and church by personal contacts where love and acceptance can be given and received enabled by the Holy Spirit.

The words sounded great, but we did not yet realize what would be required to make them come to life.

Our next challenge was to choose the persons who would participate. Through our contacts with the prison at Christmas, there were already a dozen persons from the church interested in more involvement. The six who eventually began were those who had some experience in our small Christian Growth Groups.[1] In these groups we sought to listen carefully, involve everyone in discussion, and accept every comment as having value. These were persons who made no apology for their personal Christian faith but who were sensitive to other points of view. Without the faithfulness of these original six, the group would have never survived to the point where others could follow in their place.

The chaplain worked with Jim and Nelson in selecting eight men from the prison. These were men who had showed an interest in the program and who had at least six months before they could be released. Of necessity this was an arbitrary process in a prison of 1,600 men, but those eight have a special place in our thoughts. In my mind I think of their real names, but in this book they are Jim, Nelson, Ben, Clark, Sonny, Dan, Jake, and Jeff. Many more were to come after them.

As we came to our first meeting, we found that it was not the same as gathering in someone's living room for a church meeting. There were delays at locked doors, inspections by guards, and a tiny, stuffy room. Nevertheless, there seemed to be the same intense interest that we had experienced during the Christmas program.

As the weeks passed, we found that the delays and administrative details of prison life constantly robbed us of our time together. We struggled with this problem at every turn in order to save as much as possible of our allotted two hours in the prison for dialogue with the men. Some of this time was used to gather in smaller groups of two or four, since quieter persons were often left out of the discussions in the larger group. We found it very important to use the first part of our meetings as a time when the inmates could share what had happened to them since we last met. With personal, legal, and family needs on their minds, it was important for us to deal with these before talking about the topic for the evening.

Our topics came from many sources. Sometimes the sharing of personal history by someone in the group provided a natural and urgent subject. At other times current events in or out of the prison became the discussion topic. Occasionally we used an "interest finder" to discover relevant topics. We customarily began each meeting with some related Scripture in order to provide insight and direction for our discussions.

Some of our discussion topics were:

What do you do with resentment?

How can you know that you're worth something?

Why do the wicked prosper?

How do you handle dope and booze?

Can you die "before your time"? (This was suggested by a man who had been on "death row.")

What about the Black Muslims?

Can a Christian lose his temper?

How far do you go with forgiveness?

As the months passed, we began to call those who came in from the outside "outmates" not in contrast to, but as a link with "inmates." We also decided to relate to the Yokefellow Prison Ministry[2] so as to give the group contact with a larger fellowship of concerned persons. This also provided for fellowship with Yokefellow groups on the outside when inmates were released. During this time a few other churches sent visitors to see what we were doing. One of those, the Lower Providence Baptist Church, had two of its members become a faithful part of the group. One other development was an extra meeting every third month to which we could invite a limited number of outside guests. Occasionally, a resource person would be invited to speak on topics, such as parole, community treatment centers, or Yokefellow International. This special meeting usually included refreshments and a time for socializing.

We made some discoveries about leadership in our first months of meeting. First, we discovered that some persons tended to monopolize the discussion, and a leader was needed to keep us on the subject and to make sure that each person had opportunity to speak. This leadership was usually rotated among the members of the group. Second, we discovered that many of the inmates had leadership skills. We learned that for persons who grew up in the ghettos, leadership skills are often necessary for survival.

One inmate took an interest in publishing a newssheet for our group which was circulated in the prison and the church. In one issue he listed his own perception of the purposes of the group:

To establish a positive relationship between residents and the community, and to promote resident personal and social responsibility.

To counteract the fear, apathy, prejudice, and indifference that is prevalent within the community in regard to those imprisoned; also, to counteract community hostility toward residents upon their release.

To create a climate of awareness and sensitivity within the community of our humanity and of our plight bearing the stigma of convicted men; as we, the convicted, seek to change and rehabilitate ourselves with the understanding and support of the churches and the community.

*Meanwhile . . . back at the church*—If this ministry truly was to be an extension of the local church, it seemed important to us that the total congregation be informed as to what was happening. In an effort to do this, we placed articles in our church's newsletter as well as in the local paper. We also made brief reports from time to time in the worship service. A special program was planned on a Sunday evening when the superintendent of the prison was invited to speak to the church. A time for questions followed.

After about a year, we felt that it was important to have a firm commitment of support from the total congregation. We also felt that others ought to know ways in which they could get involved. We asked for official and full support from the congregation and shared with them specific proposals for involvement.[3] The church gave a clear consensus of its support.

Despite this supportive resolution there were church members who were not pleased with this ministry. A few of them personally expressed their disapproval to me, believing this was not a proper activity for the pastor or church members. I responded by clarifying our purposes and sharing what I understood about our mission as Christians. Looking back at that stage, I realize how incomplete my response must have been.

However, this was not a divisive experience for our church, and we continued to sense the prayerful support of the congregation. That support kept us going when what we had planned began to fall apart. As the "honeymoon" period passed, problems began to surface that were to challenge all our purposes and assumptions.

### CHAPTER 2

# The Way It Almost Ended

Since we knew that redemptive change did not come without its problems in the local church, we did not expect it to be otherwise in prison. However, we were not prepared for either the intensity or the types of problems we encountered.

While the administration of the prison was originally sympathetic to our experiment, community objection to "liberal" prison programs and a change in administration cooled this support. We came to have less and less freedom to follow through on our goals. Visitors in the group were limited; social contacts beyond the group prohibited; and security measures became more apparent. This more "uptight" atmosphere in the prison obviously did not help in breaking down walls of distrust within the group.

Nor did it take us long to discover that prisons were not built to provide an environment for discussion, meditation, clear thinking, or comfort. Our room was ugly, uncomfortable, stuffy, and crowded. We became accustomed to dealing with air conditioners that didn't work, windows that wouldn't open, radiators that were either too hot or cold, and many interruptions. "Visitor for 3989." "Is 0325 in here?" "You can't use this room tonight." The bars on the windows were not nearly as distracting as the noise that seeps into every corner of a prison.

There were problems unfolding in the group itself. One would think that inmates would be a captive audience. They were not. A few were released, and others exercised their prerogative to leave the group if they felt it did not meet their needs. Lee was one of those who left.

Lee was tall, good-looking, friendly, and easily likable. That was part of the problem; it was hard to say "no" to Lee when he asked for a favor. The favor sometimes consisted of mailing a letter or bringing in a book. Sometimes we had to turn Lee down because we felt that what he asked violated prison rules. Then, for no apparent reason, he dropped out of the group. We later learned that he had been involved in a number of attempts to use people from the outside as couriers for contraband.

This illustrated one of our most serious problems, that of manipulation. Given the unreal environment of prison, the difficulty most inmates had in facing reality before being confined, and the passionate desire of all normal men to get out of prison by any means, efforts at manipulation should not have been surprising to us. One style of manipulation is commonly known as "conning," which is defined as "persuading by deception or cajolery."[1] Since it is a form of deception, "conning" was a barrier to any personal growth. There was a continual need to be sensitive to this, confront it, and bring as much honesty as possible to all relationships. It came to be a deeper problem than any of us had imagined.

Outmates, too, dropped out. Mark and Angela[2] were a delightful young couple who seemed to feel this ministry was their calling. Newly married, they added a definite zest to the group. Because our purpose included a ministry of deeds as well as words, there were many times when the act of calling a family member or appearing at a hearing became a breakthrough in an inmate's relationship with the outmates. We could not do everything they asked, but we could do some of the things they asked. It was natural, then, for an inmate to assume that such concern would continue upon his release. But for Mark and Angela what seemed to be a safe involvement with a man inside the prison became a threatening involvement when he was outside. When one of the previous group members, now on parole, called their home to ask for some assistance, they withdrew from all involvement with the group. It was a disappointing experience and made the rest of us wonder how far we would be willing to go in *our* involvement. Would it go beyond prison walls?

Ours was one of only two programs within the prison that included women, and this, too, presented some problems. The prison administration and especially the guards had fears about allowing women into the prison. These men were often desperately lonely, but we never found the inmates in our group anything but gentlemen. However, some of the correspondence with women outmates indicated that we needed continually to clarify the purpose for which we had become involved. Because of this situation we decided to have women participate in the group only if their husbands were also able to be participants. We felt that this created a more normal setting and helped the inmates express their feelings about their own families.

We had many occasions to discover just how crucial these family ties were for the men. For instance, Joel was one of the first men in our group to get a furlough weekend outside the prison. Before he left, we felt that Joel was developing the self-confidence he needed as he accepted God's love for himself. Joel had not been home for years and was greatly looking forward to the encouragement a reunion with his family would bring. He did not return to the group following the furlough weekend. We found out that while at home he learned for the first time that his son was also in prison. This was devastating to him, and his self-confidence and spiritual growth were temporarily crushed.

There were other things that so preoccupied a person's thoughts that he could not relate to the group. Burt attended the group for many weeks and always managed to turn the conversation around to his problems with getting parole. We treated this as a legitimate need and did what we felt we could in contacting his caseworker and his judge. It was not enough for Burt. He grew hostile and dropped out because he could not concentrate on anything else.

Outmates also had their own consuming needs. Pete felt "called" to take on the prison group as his special kind of ministry. However, he was used to equating success with visible and measurable results. As the months passed, he found no way to measure success and, instead, often encountered disappointments. His personal need to be associated with "successful" projects caused him to drop out with the comment "Nothing is being accomplished here." We did not want to believe Pete's words, but the following experiences made them come back to haunt us!

Jim was one of the most promising members of our group. He had worked with the chaplain on the original selection committee and seemed a wise counselor to his fellow inmates. We followed and supported Jim through the process of furlough, work release, parole, and the reestablishment of family ties on the outside. A church member helped him find a job upon release, and Jim was often a guest in our homes and at worship. Gradually our contacts grew less frequent. Then one day we saw him again—back in Graterford Prison. We knew the odds were about 50-50 that the average released prisoner would be back—but Jim was hardly average. He had everything going for him. So we thought. Jim's return made us realize that we did not yet understand the difficulty and pain of change in prison.

Finally, there was Mike. He was a prize. He taught us all how to listen. For example, one evening Chuck, whose story introduced this book, began to unload a lot of hostility on the rest of the group. Chuck announced that our program was a waste of time for him. Many of us responded by attacking Chuck's reasoning and pointing out how much good the group had done for him. But Mike was not so insensitive. He told us to be quiet and turned to Chuck and asked, "*Why* do you feel the group is a waste of time for you?" By this sympathetic question Mike took Chuck off the defensive and let him know that we wanted to hear him out. In the moments that followed, Chuck was able to reveal some of the deeper sources of his hostility. This went far beyond our group, back to a father, a wife, and even children who he felt had rejected him.

Many other times Mike listened "between the lines" hearing the pain or the deeper problem that lay beneath the surface of the spoken word. Even though Mike did not profess to be a Christian, he taught us how to listen as Christians. As the time came for Mike to leave, many expressed the feeling that they would miss his help. Mike left the prison—and within weeks shot a policeman while stealing $20.

Where had we gone wrong? Pondering all that had happened, we wondered whether this ministry was a response to God's call or just our own efforts at being "do-gooders." We had become painfully aware of our limitations. We either had to search for and find clear foundations for this ministry or give it up. The next chapter is the beginning of that search for foundations.

# CHAPTER 3

# Driven to the Scriptures

We began to ask ourselves, "Why did we, as Christians who enjoyed the routine of our neighborhood church, ever enter the door of a prison?"

We decided that ultimately it was due to this same troublesome Book that has continually broken the comfortable routine of Christians. Did not the Bible command us to take the Good News of redemption to the uttermost parts of the world? Were not today's prisons as "uttermost" as Tibet in their own way?

However, we also had now come to realize that unless those who make this journey to prison have deep scriptural and theological roots, little fruit could be expected. We now knew that a prison setting was a hostile environment and that weak or uninformed motives would not be sufficient for survival. L. Alexander Harper reaches the same conclusions as we did as to the need for biblical roots:

> Many people have wondered why Christian congregations far from jails and penitentiaries get mixed up in prison reform. Is it, they wonder, only another busybody meddling? Or a new way for jaded suburbanites to get their kicks, dramatizing their superiority and trickling a bit of pity to the poor unfortunates incarcerated in prisons?
>
> For some participants, perhaps. But others find they simply cannot continue aloof from the world's prisoners without intolerable self-contradiction in a church whose Lord was himself imprisoned as a felon, convicted as a subversive, and executed between thieves.
>
> They know that the chosen text for Jesus' first sermon was the call of Isaiah to bring "the opening of prison to those who are bound." [Luke 4:18]

They know that his simplest test for discipleship included this norm, "I was in prison and you visited me" [Matthew 25:36], with the reminder that any treatment or neglect of those scorned or punished was similar treatment and neglect of him.

They know the haunting admonition of the Letter to the Hebrews: "Remember those in prison as if you were there with them; and those who are being maltreated, for you like them are still in the world" (Hebrews 13:3, NEB).[1]

As a pastor I could see that preaching at the traditional Sunday afternoon service could no longer be regarded as a complete fulfillment either of a prison ministry or of our mission to take the Good News of Christ's redemption to the prisoner. Yet our failures forced us to look more deeply into the Scripture. In doing so, we discovered at least six motives and directions for a prison ministry:

1. "The Mark of Cain"—a biblical basis for the value of the criminal.
2. "Prisoner as Prophet"—a biblical basis for listening to prisoners.
3. "All Have Sinned"—a biblical basis for our common need.
4. "Accountability and Responsibility"—a biblical basis for our common judgment.
5. "The Nature of Grace"—a biblical basis for our common hope.
6. "Inasmuch . . ."—a final biblical imperative.

## "THE MARK OF CAIN"—
## A BIBLICAL BASIS FOR THE VALUE OF THE CRIMINAL

The story of Cain in Genesis 4:1-16 is important because it represents one of the most ancient biblical traditions as to the treatment of criminals. It is an unusual passage because, unlike later portions of the Old Testament, the death sentence is not invoked for a serious crime.

Cain was punished, not by death, but rather by exile. This is the same punishment meted out to Adam and Eve in response to the first crime against God. In these passages, the Bible describes criminals as persons to be saved rather than objects to be destroyed. God's dealings with Cain set important precedents for the treatment of criminals, and they are worth looking at in greater detail.

*First*, we note that the setting of the crime is in the context of a larger society than just the family group indicated in verse 1, for in verse 14 Cain is concerned about the punishment he will receive from society as a whole, not just from a family group. This is important because it means that in this account we are dealing with the consequences of criminal behavior not in a small family or primitive tribe—but in organized society. It has a message for our time.

*Second,* we note that this Scripture is full of high emotion. Cain was jealous of his brother and visibly angry. God responded with great concern, trying to cool him down with assurance that the future could be different. If he did well, he, too, would be accepted. But Cain's emotions had the best of him and these emotions threatened to consume Cain like an animal. The Scripture indicates that Cain killed in a jealous rage. The motive was as simple and as dangerous as jealousy. Today, a passion-filled encounter is the setting for most murders. We think of the murderer as the worst of all criminals; we give him or her the longest sentences. Statistics would show, however, that the vast majority of murders happen just as in Cain's case—in a fit of passion often involving a friend, spouse, or relative. Jealousy, anger, and hatred are experienced by all people, not just hardened criminals. Who of us knows how much pressure we can take and, given certain conditions, who knows what passion might lead us to do? This does not in any way excuse Cain, as he tried to excuse himself, but it helps us see the feelings we have in common with Cain and the similar feelings experienced by those who hurt others in a moment of passion. Cain's story could be our story. There, but for the grace of God, could go any one of us.

*Third,* Cain had to face the consequences of his crime. God allowed no passing of the buck, no extenuating circumstances. It was a crime of passion and as such represented a weakness found in all, but that did not mitigate its damning results. God insisted that Cain accept the responsibility for his act. It is the same today.

*Fourth,* the sentence of Cain, described in verse 12, was hard but not hopeless. Life would be difficult, but not impossible. Cain responded to the sentence in a revealing way. He apparently could cope with the exile and the difficulty of earning a living. God's sentence was just and had the potential for the refining of his nature. It was the sentence from his peers that seemed hopeless to

Cain. He expressed the feeling that a lifetime of fearing human revenge was an impossible prospect. Today we have not yet realized that long periods of fear can only destroy any chance for a new way of life.

*Fifth,* we see that God gives hope. It cannot be said too often that God's justice always includes hope. Without hope there is no chance for redemption—a new way of responding to life. God gave hope to Cain by placing a mark on him that would tell everyone that he was under God's protection. God is not so small that he must take revenge. He is in the business of saving life, not destroying it.

This idea of protection after punishment is also seen in the history of the Hebrew nation in the idea of the "cities of refuge" (see Joshua 20). This concept provided a cooling off period so that God's kind of justice, and not human revenge, could come into play. The horns of the altar of God were also supposed to be a place of refuge for those fleeing the vengeance of men (1 Kings 2:28). We can see in the Old Testament the mercy as well as the justice of God that Jesus brought to full flower. The main point of this dialogue between Holy God and a sinful murderer is that Cain was regarded as having value. The mark was given to preserve that value, a mark of hope for the future.

This manner of dealing with the criminal is not a soft view of criminal behavior, because life under God's chastisement is sometimes harder to bear than death. The important difference is that, unlike death, which removes all hope, God's chastisement can have a redemptive purpose. Where there is life, there is hope, and hope is indispensable to redemption. The basic lesson of Cain is to teach us that God is in the business of saving persons (even killers), not destroying them. This theme is repeated many times in the New Testament in Scriptures like John 3:17: "For God sent the Son into the world, not to condemn the world, but that the world might be saved through him."

It seems necessary to call attention to this point because many Christians still call for capital punishment as part of the solution to criminal behavior and believe that if more prisoners were executed instead of paroled, the crime problem would be on its way to solution. Arguing the statistics about the value of capital punishment is beside the point for Christians. If God preserved the life of a confessed murderer, if this is his style of justice in one of the most basic traditions of the biblical record, then it seems that we ought to regard every criminal as a person of value. Churches and individual Christians will never be able to play a redemptive role among prisoners until they believe that the mark of Cain is a mark of preservation and not of destruction.

Unfortunately, in our current vocabulary the mark of Cain is a mark of disapprobation, an evil mark, a curse. It is not so in this original context; here it is a mark of hope and salvation. That seems to illustrate the contemporary problem of Christians and prisoners. We see them as under a curse. God sees them with a mark of hope.

## "THE PRISONER AS PROPHET"—
## A BIBLICAL BASIS FOR LISTENING TO PRISONERS

The story of Cain teaches us that criminals are to be preserved with hope. The Bible goes further; it tells us that the prisoner may be God's prophet. To make this easier for us to accept, we should first realize that the prisoners mentioned in the Bible are almost always the "good guys"! From Joseph to John, from Genesis to Revelation, God's prophets are found in Egyptian dungeons and lonely islands of exile. Today it is easier for us to believe that Jeremiah or Paul spoke from prison as God's prophets than to believe this of a contemporary prisoner. However, we need to remember that it was probably as difficult for contemporaries of the biblical prophets to accept their word of the Lord from prison as it is for us today to accept the word of God from a Martin Luther King, Jr., in the Birmingham jail or a George Jackson in Soledad Prison.

The prisoner as a prophet is a familiar figure in history, especially biblical history. Therefore, we have reason to listen carefully in our own generation. For instance, Peter went to jail because he and the apostles said, "We must obey God rather than men" (Acts 5:29). In our day there are people who were jailed because they said the same thing about their refusal to kill people in Vietnam.

Jeremiah had a message from God to deliver to his nation. Because of his stubborn faithfulness to that message, he was imprisoned by the authorities of that nation (see Jeremiah 37). The story of Martin Luther King, Jr., is not dissimilar.

Yet it is fair to say that most prison inmates do not parallel the biblical prophets in this more obvious way. There are other ways to be prophetic, symbolized in a person like George Jackson. Certainly Jackson professed no Christian faith; yet biblical insights were part of his training.[2] As he raged against society, he voiced something many of us suspected but did not wish to face. He pointed to us as a violent society full of destructive forces, and he warned of the wrath to come.[3] In effect he both announced and was fulfilling Jesus' prophecy that "All who take the sword will perish by the sword" (Matthew 26:52). A violent society helped to produce George Jackson and thousands of other prisoners like him. This is not to take away their personal responsibility but to see the prophetic dimension of their angry words. George Jackson was a dangerous man, a man who is difficult for us to understand, but he and others who are voicing anger are holding up a mirror to our society much as the biblical prophets did. What they see shows us to be wanting not only in our system of justice but also in the sociological, psychological, and spiritual wisdom that can keep us from continually creating such violent men.

The biblical prophets were recognized as such because they were people who heard a message society couldn't hear, who saw things their culture could not see, and who proclaimed ideas that their contemporaries often did not want to know. Sometimes gentle, like Martin Luther King, Jr., sometimes angry like George Jackson, there are contemporary prisoners saying things that society and Christians need to hear whether we wish to or not. These who are often from disenfranchised minorities and separated from most Christians in many ways can alert us to realities that we urgently need to see.

Not every prisoner is God's prophet, but to fail to be open to this possibility is to fail to learn the lessons of the Bible. To have this openness also helps keep one from the patronizing attitude that cripples most Christian efforts at prison ministry. Just being aware that God can and might speak a word through the prisoner could help change this ministry from a duty to an opportunity. It is always helpful to remember that most of the New Testament was written by a "jailbird" (Paul), and his subject was a crucified, convicted criminal!

## "ALL HAVE SINNED"—
## A BIBLICAL BASIS FOR OUR COMMON NEED

When we have learned that God seeks to give hope to the criminal through the mark of Cain and may even speak a word through the prisoner as His prophet, we have learned basically Old Testament lessons.

The New Testament deals with even more radical concepts: our common sin, judgment, and hope.

We are in the habit of using the word "criminal" in its contemporary sense as one who breaks the law. The New Testament teaches that all persons break the law of God and thus removes such niceties of distinction as that between the "criminal" and the "rest of us." We are able to accept Paul as a prophet because, while he was a prisoner, he supposedly was not a criminal. Conversely, we find it difficult to accept George Jackson as a prophet because he was both. Paul, who himself had once consented to murder (Acts 8:1-3), will not let us make that distinction and tells us, "all have sinned" and "the wages of sin is death" (Romans 3:23; 6:23). To sin against God is a crime; all persons are sinners; all are criminals! The implications of this are most uncomfortable. Somehow it does not seem as bad for us to be sinners as it is to be criminals; yet the New Testament says they are one and the same!

In Romans, chapter 3, Paul compares Jew and Gentile, and instead of debating which group is better off in God's sight, he brings all to the same level by saying, "Jews and Gentiles alike are all under the power of sin" (Romans 3:9, TEV) and concludes this passage by stating that his purpose for writing is "to stop all human excuses and bring the whole world under God's judgment" (Romans 3:19, TEV).

James in his plain way indicts us all as criminals, "Whoever breaks one command of the Law is guilty of breaking them all" (James 2:10, TEV). James brings out the biblical truth that God does not see sin as a particular act, but as a state of rebellion. This rebellion manifests itself in different ways with different people, but all have a common need of reconciliation with God that overshadows the weighing or measuring of sin or criminality.

The New Testament strips all glamour and justification from sin in any of its forms. To defraud a stockholder requires the same careless attitude toward the worth of others as does rape. Our legal system has not been able to accept this radical understanding of sin; so we send the murderer to prison for life, the robber for a few years, and the corrupt lawyer for a few days. When the disciples asked Jesus about the relation of crime to punishment, they were looking for a carefully matched equation. Jesus replied, "If you do not turn from your sins, you will all die as they did" (Luke 13:5, TEV). With Jesus there was no distinction between bad sins and those not so bad; there was only sin committed by sinners worthy of death and in need of forgiveness.

A group of Christians who had become concerned with the Essex County Jail (New Jersey) expressed their motivation in this way:

> Our interest in the Essex County Jail cannot be put on the basis of "doing something for the unfortunate." Rather, it is based on the sheer awareness that under God there is no difference between those in jails and those who are not. We give our attention to the jailed not in any disinterested way, but as fellow prisoners with them.[4]

Most of us brought up in the church know this in our heads. We have been told that it is as wrong to lust after a woman as to commit adultery and it is as wrong to shade the truth on our income tax as it is to steal, but we persist in living as if the prisoner were a worse kind of sinner than those of us on the outside.

Karl Menninger sees something of the biblical concept of the scapegoat in our attitude toward offenders:

> . . . society secretly *wants* crime, *needs* crime, and gains definite satisfactions from the present mishandling of it! We condemn crime; we punish offenders for it; but we need it. . . . We need crimes to wonder at, to enjoy vicariously, to discuss and speculate about, and to publicly deplore. We need criminals to identify ourselves with, to secretly envy, and to stoutly punish. . . . They do for us the forbidden, illegal things we *wish* to do and, like scapegoats of old, they bear the burdens of our displaced guilt and punishment. . . .[5]

Menninger touches a very deep nerve here. Before we dismiss his words as an overstatement, we need to examine our own hearts and ponder the words of Jesus which cut deeply into the self-righteousness of his listeners. "Let him who is without sin among you be the first to throw a stone . . ." (John 8:7).

Yes, there are actions the state needs to take for the public safety. Yes, persons who willfully hurt others ought to be punished. But

Christians ought to check their zeal for vengeance against the probing psychological and spiritual insights of our Lord. There is much darkness in our own hearts for which the cross is a vivid reminder.

To come into a prison setting with any shade of superiority is not only a patronizing attitude easily detected by inmates, but it is also not true to the Scriptures. Until we accept the radical New Testament teaching of our common sin, until we understand that we are simply beggars telling other beggars where we have found bread, we cannot be a redemptive influence anywhere.

## "ACCOUNTABILITY AND RESPONSIBILITY"— A BIBLICAL BASIS FOR OUR COMMON JUDGMENT

One of the reasons we find it difficult to face our common sin is that it seems to minimize personal responsibility. Certainly in the light of recent political scandals prisoners are feeling more and more justified in saying, "Everybody does it . . . I just happened to get caught," or "I just couldn't afford a high-powered lawyer," or "I just had the misfortune to be black instead of white."

There is truth in all these statements and they point out situations that cry for reform in our systems of justice. However, the smugness that says "everybody does it" is not a step of healing or redemption for those either in or out of prison.

As Christians in dialogue with a prison community, we can sympathize with the failures of our system of justice; we can admit that we too are sinners. But if we stop there, we are only bleeding hearts with little redemptive hope to offer. Compassion and understanding are needed; coddling and excuses are not.

The biblical record reveals a God who is concerned, not with excuses, but to change the way in which we respond and act now. He knew that Moses, Daniel, Peter, and the others he chose had certain flaws in their character. God did not allow them to use these as excuses but demanded accountability when they failed. The scriptural picture of humanity says that we are responsible for our actions. Psychiatry may uncover all kinds of reasons that could be used to excuse our behavior; American justice may give further excuses; but the Scriptures announce that we are responsible for our actions and that we must give account to both God and society.

The story of Eve and Adam says this well (Genesis 2:15-17; 3:1-

19). As primitive as the story may be, it was preserved by the Hebrews and quoted by Jesus because it revealed an eternal truth: persons are responsible for their actions and accountable to God. The story unfolds in clear steps.

First, came the instructions from God, the Law: "And the Lord God commanded the man [woman] saying, 'You may freely eat of every tree of the garden; but of the tree of the knowledge of good and evil, you shall not eat, for in the day that you eat of it you shall die'" (Genesis 2:16-17).

Second, came the temptation. The text uses the excellent word "subtle" (Genesis 3:1) to describe the serpent. He provides the excuse we often plead—"it seemed so harmless." The suggestion of disobedience was not only subtle; it suggested that God wasn't as concerned for the pleasure of his creatures as he professed to be.

Third, came the choice. Eve was persuaded by the excuses supplied for her, and she broke the command. Adam didn't even require the subtlety of the serpent; he just mimicked his wife!

Finally, came the call to accountability. Excuses were paraded. Eve claimed that the beguiling nature of the offer had caused her to fall. Adam claimed that if his wife did it, it must be OK. Neither dared tell God that His own goodness and willingness to care for them had also been questioned.

God did not take any of the excuses into account. There were no extenuating or mitigating circumstances. The judgment was passed, and it was true to God's pattern of swiftness and hope. The consequences were to be felt immediately; yet as Adam and Eve suffered under this judgment, God gave them hope: there would be a way out. It would not be easy; but they could still know something of God's plan, yet now as exiles.

This account teaches us that human beings were created as persons who were responsible for their behavior and that they would have to give account of this behavior before God. Of equal importance is the teaching that the most persuasive excuses do not relieve us of responsibility and accountability. Just as prisoners and nonprisoners share in common sin, we also share in a common responsibility and accountability to God. Just as sin is grievous for prisoner and nonprisoner alike, excuses from responsibility are also mutually invalid before God. Persuasive arguments may be given by nonprisoners to the effect that their sin is somehow less serious than the sins of prisoners, and prisoners may persuasively argue that racism, injustice, and environment excuse them from responsibility; but none of these arguments stands up before the God of the Scriptures—all have sinned; all will come into judgment for their sin.

The kind of "bleeding-heart" mentality that will let people use the same excuses again and again to escape responsibility not only has no place in prisons, but it also inhibits any possibility for change. Only when our common need and judgment are accepted, will we be driven to God's grace. This, and not excuses, is our only hope for new life in and out of prisons.

## "THE NATURE OF GRACE"—
## A BIBLICAL BASIS FOR OUR COMMON HOPE

... an offender must be punished ... I don't argue about that. But to punish and not to restore, that is the greatest of all offenses. ...

... if a man takes unto himself God's right to punish, then he must also take upon himself God's promise to restore. ...

There's a hard law ... that when deep injury is done to us, we never recover until we forgive.[6]

One must talk about "sin" and "judgment" before one can understand "grace." Only after we have accepted the deep and tragic implications of the commonness of our sin and judgment can we appreciate the idea of grace—the unimaginable, illogical, lavish, and undeserved love that Jesus Christ brought into the world.

It is the fact that all three of these experiences—sin, judgment, and grace—are shared by prisoners and nonprisoners alike that breaks down the spiritual and social barriers between us. To speak of grace without speaking of sin and judgment is cheap sentimentality. However, to speak about sin and judgment without speaking of grace is discouraging and hopeless. In the prison community as in all places we need to hear of all three.

Grace is hard to understand because it cannot be measured. In the parable of the workers in the vineyard, the hours of labor are not related to the amount of reward (Matthew 20:1-16). Jesus teaches that rewards are given not according to some reference book where levels of deserving and undeserving are given values, but according to a graciousness and undeserved love that go beyond human standards of justice. Grace is measureless and incomputable.

I believe the most important characteristic of persons who wish to have a redemptive role in a prison setting is that they be deeply aware of how little they have deserved what God has given them. Even the fact that they are not in prison is by grace. The person who addresses a group of prisoners with the comment "I had all the disadvantages you fellows had, but by hard work and perseverance I made it" not only cuts himself off from any communication with others, but also he does not even know himself. To look at a prisoner and say, "There but for the grace of God go I" is not just a cliché; it is the truth. Paul's letters were battering rams to break down walls—walls between Jew and Gentile, slave and free, male and female. A background paper for the 184th General Assembly of the United Presbyterian Church, U.S.A., has this to say:

> The abolition of the wall of hostility between non-criminal and criminal does not proceed from an indifference to right or wrong or from paternalism. It is the worth and dignity bestowed upon persons by the creative act of God that should make us as Christians loathe to mistreat any person or class of persons because they appear to be a threat to established order. Our caution should be even the greater because we know that the systems of criminal justice reflect closely the injustice present in society's unequal distribution of power and opportunity. The Christian's desire to overcome his sin and error and his recognition of the fact that only God is good makes him more sensitive to good and to evil, but for those very reasons more aware also of the ambiguity of all human behavior. He accepts as a gift of grace his own status in society and he recognizes that God has given his grace unto all persons, both the good and the evil.[7]

The power to break these walls came from the idea of grace powerfully outlined by Paul, especially in his letter to the Ephesians. In Ephesians 2:3 (TEV) he includes himself as under God's righteous judgment. "All of us were like them, and lived according to our natural desires, and did whatever suited the wishes of our own bodies and minds. Like everyone else we, too, were naturally bound to suffer God's wrath." But in Ephesians 2:5, he declares that grace precludes all deserving; "while we were spiritually dead in our disobedience he brought us to life in Christ" (TEV). In Romans 5:8 Paul says it another way, "It was while we were still sinners that Christ died for us" (TEV). The idea of first deserving this love and forgiveness is totally absent. In the Ephesians passage Paul sums this all up by defining the word "grace" (Ephesians 2:7-9). "... by God's grace you have been saved. . . . He did this to demonstrate for all time to come the extraordinary greatness of his grace in the love he showed us in Christ Jesus. For it is by God's grace that you have saved, through faith. It is *not* your own doing, but God's gift. There is *nothing* here to boast of, since it is not the result of your own efforts" (Ephesians 2:5-9, TEV, italics added).

The person who claims his hard work and perseverance have kept him out of prison and in God's favor could never believe these verses. Our good fortune or bad is due far more to where we were born (geography and environment), who we were born (sex, race, and nationality), with what we were born (genetic characteristics), and even what we were fed (diet) than to any efforts of our own. For some this is a discouraging picture of hopelessness and predestination. For Paul and his gospel of grace it simply meant that both he who boasted of his good fortune and he who complained of his bad fortune should put away the past and live a new life. Then the only boasting would be about what God has done out of sheer, undeserved grace. Grace is the great leveler. It leads deacon and convicted murderer to stand on the same ground before God.

The grace of Jesus Christ has the wonderful property of leaving us still responsible and accountable beings even as it opens the door of forgiveness. I have often recalled the words of my seminary professor of ethics, Dr. Culbert Rutenber, that while forgiveness is freely given, "forgiveness is not a cheap and easy thing."[8]

The grace that forgives and puts the deacon and the convicted murderer on an equal footing also puts them at the foot of the cross where they can see what this grace cost.

We have spoken of the mark of Cain. It was an Old Testament mark of preservation and hope. Now we have a New Testament mark of preservation and hope for the criminal. It is the cross of Christ that opens up the way of grace through sacrificial love and forgiveness. This mark is not only needed by the likes of Cain, but also it is needed by us all. This mark of grace breaks down any barriers we can contrive: Jew and Gentile, slave and free, male and female, white and black, prisoner and nonprisoner.

## "INASMUCH . . ."—
## A FINAL BIBLICAL IMPERATIVE

Jesus' picture of the Final Judgment as found in Matthew 25:31-46 is one of the most disturbing sections of the Bible. It outlines a style of life that takes the Christian into some unpleasant places . . . where people are starving . . . dying of thirst . . . in the midst of strangers . . . to the naked . . . among the sick . . . even into prisons.

As I lay this standard beside my life and the life of my church, I feel very uncomfortable. We do not measure up as we should. We who have undeservedly received the measureless grace of God are expected to have the kind of mission Jesus outlines here. But instead of feeding the hungry, we build additions to our sanctuaries; instead of offering drink to the thirsty, we work on innovative worship services; instead of reaching out to strangers, we seek out those who are like ourselves; instead of clothing the naked, we rebuild our organ; instead of caring for the sick, we send flowers; instead of visiting the prisoner . . . ? As one fellow pastor said, "The whole subject of prisons is a problem in my church. It just creates a hassle; so I avoid it." That is what most of us do when it comes to prisons. We avoid the subject; it saves hassles. But how can we avoid a clear command of Jesus? To water down the command is the same as disobeying it. I do not think that a worship service in the prison auditorium once a year fulfills a church's responsibility. I do not think impersonal contacts of this nature are what Jesus had in mind. He said, "*I* was in prison and you visited *me.*" What could be more personal?

In spite of the biblical imperatives described in this chapter, I wonder if they will change any minds. Perhaps, however, these words of Jesus can break through our blindness and fears. No one wants to visit murderers, rapists, junkies, and thieves, much less become involved with them; but what Christian would fail to visit, care for, and minister to Jesus Christ?

These are exactly the terms on which our Lord invites us to a ministry within prison walls. He is there; and if we have cared about anyone there, we have cared for Him. "Whenever you did this for one of the least important of these brothers of mine, you did it for me!" (Matthew 25:40, TEV). As uncomfortable as these verses make me and my church feel, and as difficult as it is to look on a three-time loser in maroon prison pants as the Christ, I'm glad this imperative is in the Bible. Someday I may be that "least important brother" and I'll know that He has left a command with His people to care for me.

### CHAPTER 4

# Learning About Prisons

As we shared the biblical insights of the previous chapter with one another, we began to see our failures in a different perspective. It was possible that we were where we were behind prison walls not to succeed but to obey. We had made mistakes, but we could not yet feel that it was time to quit; rather, it was time to be better informed and motivated. We came to realize that after studying the Bible, we had to know more about prison itself. We had to know more about what happened to prisoners in the hundreds of hours that surrounded the precious two hours we spent with them.

I can't tell you what the "soul" of a prison is like. Only someone who has been a prisoner can tell you that. But for those who will search, there is much to be learned *about* prisons in America.

The most striking thing is that we have lots of prisons and prisoners in America: more than four thousand prisons of various types.[1] Approximately 90 percent of the church members in America are within an hour's drive of one of these prisons. We don't often see the buildings that house these people because we don't look for them. For the most part they are unattractive, old, and out of the way.

Yet it is not the number, location, or appearance that describes a prison, but the people within. Most inmates are men; most are young (over half under 30);[2] and most are from minority groups. This latter fact does not mean that minority groups inherently behave worse than others, only that they receive more and longer prison sentences. The most critical statistic is that almost all prisoners will be released, usually within five years.

Yet the best definition of prisons is neither a description nor a statistic. It is a word—"failure." An ex-inmate speaking on the NBC "Today" show said, "You might as well say cologne cures gangrene as to say prisons rehabilitate people . . . prisons teach people how to do time. You can't socialize someone in prison."[3] This former inmate used the words "rehabilitate" and "socialize," but he meant the same thing that penologists mean by "reform" and Christians might describe as "redeem." Whatever word one uses, prisons are not doing the job. They fail to rehabilitate; they fail to socialize; they fail to reform; and they most certainly fail to redeem. This is not a narrow, prejudiced opinion. It is agreed to by almost every person who knows what is happening in today's prison from the Chief Justice of the Supreme Court who says:

> We have developed systems of correction which do not correct. . . . If anyone is tempted to regard humane prison reform as "coddling criminals" let him visit a prison and talk with inmates and staff. I have visited some of the best and some of the worst prisons and have never seen any signs of "coddling," but I have seen the terrible results of the boredom and frustration of empty hours and a pointless existence.[4]

to the most angry, militant inmate who finds mayhem the only adequate expression of his wordless rage at what prison is doing to him. Administrator and administrated alike sense the tragic waste and uselessness of today's prisons. Patrick V. Murphy, Commissioner of the Police Department, City of New York, says:

> It is time for someone to shout stop; this is crazy, it does not work, it is a disaster. The criminal justice system has become a perpetual motion machine which produces no viable product at all at a staggering cost.[5]

In light of this, one must ask the question, "Why is this institution of proven failure allowed to continue?" The answer lies in the fact that much of the public still sees prisons as having the three-fold function of *revenge, protection,* and *rehabilitation.* I believe Christians should take a second look at this rationale.

The idea of taking revenge upon others is forbidden by the best insights of the Old Testament not only in the story of Cain mentioned in the previous chapter, but also in Scripture, such as Leviticus 19:18: "Don't seek vengeance. Don't bear a grudge; but love your neighbor as yourself, for I am Jehovah" (*The Living Bible*). At times the Old Testament may seem ambiguous about the morality of persons taking vengeance into their own hands, but Jesus is not ambiguous: "But I say: Don't resist violence! If you are slapped on one cheek, turn the other too" (Matthew 5:39, *The Living Bible*). Using prisons for the purpose of revenge makes society criminal. Karl Menninger has elaborated this thesis in great detail in his book, *The Crime of Punishment.*[6]

Christians should also question the purpose of protection. Former Attorney General for the United States, Ramsey Clark says:

> Under any system most prisoners will be released someday. . . . If we release persons who have the capacity for further crime, only temporary safety has been afforded. In the meanwhile, imprisonment has often increased the individual's capacity for crime.[7]

In addition, our preoccupation with protection too often comes from a sub-Christian exploitation of people's fears. Christians are supposed to be guided by a Spirit of power, not of fear (see Romans 8:15 and 2 Timothy 1:7). At present it seems necessary to confine a small percentage of violent persons for their protection and ours. However, Jesus never pointed to protection and safety as high goals for his followers.

Rehabilitation sounds more positive than revenge or protection as a rationale for prisons. Yet as prisons are presently run, rehabilitation is mainly a myth. In the opinion of Randall E. Davis, Executive Director of the Pennsylvania Prison Society, ". . . nothing works . . . even the most progressive programs in education, psychiatry and the like, have not been able to demonstrate any reduction in the rate of recidivism."[8] Currently there is a trend to forsake rehabilitative programs, as prison administrators continue to be frustrated over their seeming failures. Instead of searching for answers at a deeper level, those responsible for prison policies are moving back to the purposes of revenge and protection. In spite of the failure of prisons at rehabilitation, as long as the public believes that prisons protect them or accepts the purpose of revenge, prisons will continue to be with us and more will be built.

Those walls ten miles from our church housed hundreds of human beings, inmates and staff. As Christians we learned that we could not wait for an enlightened society to find alternatives to prisons. We would have to deal with the reality at hand. In order to know that reality better, it meant that we had to listen to those who knew more about the "soul" of prisons than we could experience in our brief visits. We also needed to know their feelings about the church. We share here the view "within the walls" as seen by administrators, guards, chaplains, and, finally, the inmates themselves.

## THE ADMINISTRATORS' VIEW

Administrators find themselves in the difficult position of having too little with which to do too big a job. A largely apathetic public and busy legislators give them little moral and financial support, while demanding better protection. A minority of the public properly expect rehabilitation to occur which is even more difficult for administrators to produce. Inmates and security staff add their pressures on administrators. As a result of these varied and often contradictory expectations, today's prison administrator finds it difficult to function effectively. Our local prison has had four superintendents or acting superintendents in five years. The lesser administrative staff has suffered a similar turnover rate. A few of these people are political appointees with questionable dedication or expertise; most are deeply concerned and well trained.

**Listen to their comments:** (All quotations without footnote citations are from personnel at the State Correctional Institution, Graterford, Pennsylvania.)

A prison term itself is enough punishment. The public thinks we ought to further apply the screw when they are here. Sensory deprivation, especially separation from personal relationships, is enough. . . . Some of the men here manipulate the system so they don't mature; these are not interested in rehabilitation. Maturity and responsibility are marks of rehabilitation. . . . My first priority is the safety of the community. My second priority is rehabilitation.

They come out worse criminals than they were when they went in. . . . If we in corrections dehumanize people, we get riots. . . . Rehabilitation is a myth—unless somehow an inmate develops a new frame of mind. . . . Crime will never be reduced until the whole community becomes involved in prison reform.[9]

Prisoners in my tenure of service (30 years) have changed from being about 2/3 white and a relatively quiet population, to almost 90% black, some of whom are organizers of opposition. Today's prisoner is quite different from the prisoner of a generation ago and so are prisons. Prisons ought to be more concerned with the individual and his rehabilitation, but given the case histories of some of these men, rehabilitation seems impossible. . . . I have to care about how the surrounding community feels about us. I am most concerned about the crime situation; 90% of crimes by blacks are against blacks. That hurts me and my family. I want to do something about that.

We're charged with conflicting responsibilities—keeping convicted felons away from the "good people" and, at the same time, in the unbelievably unnatural society that prevails in prison, rehabilitating them.[10]

[Churches are] interested in the men as human beings and they show it. That's just what most inmates haven't had enough of. . . . Leaders from the community should come into the prison—not just to gape—but to offer constructive programs to afford inmates some human dignity. . . . Clergy are particularly qualified because of their education and experience with the problems of troubled people.[11]

The church's role in prisons used to be one of diversion for men who had no radio or TV or much outside contact. Now, with the exception of certain musical groups, most prisoners are not interested in a chapel service. The Black Muslims have also had an influence by discouraging fellow blacks from participating in the "white man's religion." While I am a Christian myself and want the stabilizing influence of the churches, I have certain reservations about church participation within a prison. Most of these men have been manipulating all their lives. They don't like to talk to us because we won't let them manipulate. They know that a middle-class white churchman is more likely to be manipulated. People from the churches need to know what is going on or else they can be used, and, when they discover this, they are disillusioned. This doesn't help anyone. I'm glad to have churches involved, but they and other outside groups will have to prove their value. Some white middle-class people seem to get some kind of kick out of contact with prisoners. I want people from the churches to have a better motivation than that.

I recently attended a conference on "Blacks and the Criminal Justice System." The church was not even mentioned. This makes me wonder about its role in the past. In the future I would like to see the church become an "agent for re-acceptance" in the community. One area that churches have done very little with is the concern for an imprisoned man's family. Often they are a part of his problem. I would like to see qualified people from the churches meet in the visiting room with a prisoner and his family and help them work out some of their problems.

## THE GUARDS' VIEW

Guards (security personnel) are in a position almost as difficult as administrators. The inmates with whom guards must work closely are angry people for a multitude of reasons. This anger can find very few outlets in prison. The guards, or "hacks," as they are known among inmates, are convenient objects of that anger. On the other side, their bosses, the administrators, expect them to maintain order with a minimum of fuss and hassle.

Who are the men we place in this difficult position? After the Attica riots it was learned that this facility, with a large majority of its population black or Puerto Rican, had an all-white staff of guards. While many prison systems are trying to remedy this imbalance, it still is common. In addition to usually being of a different race, most guards are not required to have specialized training. Because of the salary level, few who have any education beyond high school are attracted to this difficult and sometimes distasteful work.

Yet some stay who are both sensitive to human needs and able to enforce the necessary discipline. Some guards even earn the grudging respect of the inmates. "I spent four years in solitary for stabbing a 'hack,' but in this prison I met J. O. and this man is a gentleman!" The inmate who said this to me clearly felt that guards like this were too rare. They are rare because it is hard to survive as this kind of guard. "An officer who cares is in trouble—some inmates will take advantage of him and most guards will hate his method—he will be destroyed." This comment of another inmate reveals the reason guards so seldom dare to be any more than custodians of human cattle. Most share the feelings of one guard who said, "These guys have nothing to do twenty-four hours a day but think how to give you a hard time." Unfortunately the

inmates usually feel that the guards have the same attitude.
**Listen to their comments:**

I like my work here [a guard in the treatment section]. I had not missed a day in twenty years; last month I had an accident and the doctor told me I would have to miss a few days of work. . . . I cried. Inmates here need to have to help themselves; about half of them don't want to. . . . You can't be a guard if you can't say "no." I do what I can for the guys. I tell them, "You have to know you're going to make it. You have to have confidence in yourself." I do what I can for the guys . . . after all, we all do wrong.

I've been working in corrections thirty-two years. Things have gotten worse in the last few years—no clear rules. You have to be careful at all times.

This is an interesting job and a secure one as long as you learn it and do it. I know it's a necessary job, not the best kind of job but necessary.

I think the churches can help men, but not if it's just a social visit. They must also realize that security is most important and ladies should always have a special escort. If the men get to know some people in the churches while they're here, then when they get out they'll have someone to call when they get depressed. These men all know right from wrong. It helps when a church group brings out their problems because they learn from each other's problems. They have to know they can trust you. Once they find out you told someone else what was said in the group, they won't be back. Not many men come to the Protestant services, but the chapel is full for the Black Muslim services on Tuesday nights.

What are churches doing in here? They don't belong in prison, especially women; they're in danger. Everyone tries to help the same guys; they're a clique. Why aren't the churches interested in the rest of the men besides those the chaplain recommends? The chaplains don't do much for the men anyway. The church should worry about [crime] prevention and not come in here. The only outside group that does a good job is A.A. I always have to worry about some guy putting a knife to the throat of one of you and making you a hostage.

## THE CHAPLAINS' VIEW

The chaplains also find themselves in a double bind in the prison system. The inmates feel that the chaplains should be aggressive advocates for their needs, and administrators usually feel they should be a pacifying force in the system, meeting pastoral needs and no more. The Reverend Byron E. Eshelman tried to emphasize the "advocate" role and after twenty years of the chaplaincy at San Quentin observed, "They [the administration] see me as a saboteur. But this is just the kind of person we should have here—one who doesn't believe in this monstrosity." Mr. Eshelman further comments, "The state tries to sustain chaplains who will be beholden to the purposes of the state, but the chaplain who knows who he is isn't working for the state. The chaplain who can be bought is a phony, and that chaplain will be rejected by the inmates." [12]

This is a serious problem for chaplains, and this conflict of loyalties between service to the inmates who are their "parish" and service to the state (administrator) which is their employer is currently the subject of much debate. David Janzen, former editor of *Liberty to the Captives,* a magazine sponsored by the Mennonite Central Committee Peace Section, believes state-employed chaplains are a contradiction in ministry.

> Why, we should ask, is it in the state's interest to hire prison chaplains? One central reason is stated by the Tennessee Commissioner of Corrections, Mark Luttrell: "Nervous and mental strain in an institution is often caused by worry by inmates who fear for the welfare of their families back home. The chaplain devotes much of his time to these problems. He seems to help the inmate to find peace through freedom from prison tensions and a closer relationship with God." What is going on here? First you cage up a man, isolate him from family and community, and then you hire a man of God to help him accept his suffering and to keep the lid on the place. Is this what Jesus was about? [13]

Yet a chaplain in the Philadelphia area stated what he believed to be a consensus among his fellow chaplains:

> We have come to the conclusion that whether a man is paid by the state or by the churches is not the crucial factor in his ministry. We feel that if a man has a commitment to his calling from God and to people, he'll do a courageous job in prison. Who pays him is not going to change this.

The debate continues as prison chaplains try to define their role and minister with integrity under difficult circumstances.

**Listen to their comments:**

Prisons have a "knee-jerk" reaction to any criticism. The slightest suggestion that they are to blame for a problem brings a quick response. Truthfully, the prison isn't to blame for many problems; most problems existed before the men got here. Prisons don't destroy hope; most men feel hopeless before they get here.

My observation over the six years as prison Chaplain is that younger men who become guards are sharp, compassionate, and concerned about the men. But either they quit in a little while, beaten down by the system, or they become indoctrinated by it. Only a few endure. This is unfortunate. It takes a strong person to come in on a guard line and keep humanistic values.[14]

I have been asked what the role of the church can be in improving the treatment of the offender. I say to the church, laity, and clergy, "Get intelligently involved." I say "intelligently," because unless one is stable in his own life, he has a very hard time helping other people. Not everyone is emotionally equipped to be involved directly, but can help in indirect ways.[15]

The churches have been growing, and have so many responsibilities of their own—administrative, teaching, training. It has caused them to take their eyes off the prisoner. I hope this trend will change—it must change, in fact, if rehabilitation is to occur on a large scale.[16]

Relationship building is a definite part of the purpose of our encounter groups and many good and constructive things have been brought about by relationships begun through this experience. The members are looking for understanding, concern, insight, and acceptance which will strengthen and support them as they continue to prepare for their re-entry into society. Churches can be a part of rebuilding a life by participating in these groups.[17]

Such organizations as Yokefellow can be a help in rehabilitating offenders. If we believe that we are all sinners, and under God's judgment, and beneficiaries of his salvation, then we had better include us all. The church can urge passage of legislation aimed at more community programs. It can work for the repeal of repressive laws. It can inform itself about the needs of individual offenders and needs in improvement of the system of justice. The church can also work for smaller institutions, acceptance of work release, furloughs, and half-way houses.[18]

I can give you 52 reasons why a church is wasting its time by just holding Sunday jail services. 52's the number of prison officials and experts I talked to when I came to [this state]... and to a man they said, "We don't need more services; we need more people who will work on a one-to-one basis with inmates."[19]

The inmates just don't understand the language. The inmate is looking for an easy solution like walking down an aisle, but he doesn't realize this means he will have to change his life.[20]

Prison is nothing but a super ghetto stuffed with people who came from ghettoes, the people who have been voiceless and impotent across the years, the recipients of persecution and abuse, the scapegoats of our culture.[21]

## THE INMATES' VIEW

As noted by an administrator earlier in this chapter, prisoners have changed in the past ten or fifteen years. They are younger, angrier, more organized, and a majority are from racial minorities.

One older, white inmate told me, "What a change; I see things happening today that never could have happened before—this is crazy." This man had hated prison as much as anyone had, but at least in the past he had felt safe in the routine. His world had changed, and now he was afraid of the turmoil he felt stirring in his younger fellow-inmates of different races and cultures. They were not going to be as passive as he had been. What shocked him most was that when they banded together, as do the Black Muslims, they had real power.

Edward Bunker, a white inmate at San Quentin, writes:

> Everyone understands that Blacks have been brutalized by genera-
> tions of institutionalized racism, and recently by inertia and
> indifference. What the sympathetic fail to grasp is that sometimes the

psychological truncation is so great that it cannot be repaired. Nothing is left but hate. They have no desire—no motivation—for anything except revenge and license for whatever they desire. Additionally, they've decided that they are political prisoners. The Black realizes that he has committed a crime, or has acted against the statutes. However, the claim of "political prisoner" comes from the argument that he was formed by a corrupt system, that his acts are a result thereof, and therefore he cannot be held responsible. Secondarily, he feels that he has never been a part of this system, but is still in slavery, and consequently the White laws do not apply to him. Such personalities are often found in prison, where the flower of racism is blossoming, virulent and paranoid.[22]

Certainly not every black or minority prisoner is described here, but this is a fair description of one point of view that is shaping a new type of prisoner.

The newer prisoner has certain challenges for the church. He will ask probing questions, demand action, and have no natural inclination to hear what churches and Christians have to say.

However, many prisoners, including blacks and other minority groups, are still searching for a viable way of life. Some see unacceptable flaws in the Black Muslims and similar groups. They are at least open to give the church one more try.

**Listen to their comments:**

Everybody in jail reaches a point where he knows he doesn't want to go to jail again . . . but then the years pass—and he rots beyond that point until his hope turns to hate and you turn out a criminal.

Rehabilitation is a joke . . . if I went out and became a priest, the administration would probably say, "We rehabilitated him!" . . . Ha!

The people here didn't give me my problems; I didn't give them their problems, so why do they have to lean on me?

Guys have a right to their feelings and a right to express their feelings in a proper manner . . . even the Bible says, "be angry and sin not" so I won't let anybody keep me from being a man.

It takes a terrific amount of psychic energy to keep from hanging a towel [committing suicide] in prison. The system either lives in past or future; it's no help in the present. Prison is a warehouse; the only thing anybody wants in here is OUT. We are mostly political prisoners, prisoners of a political system that destroys the oppressed.

Vocational training is really important but only a tiny percentage get it.

Everybody who says they want to help you comes and leaves each day. Nobody has to live here; what do they know?

A riot is the only way to get things done.

When we lose our temper, we automatically learn to say, "That's the demon coming out in me," instead of saying, "That's the man coming out in me."

I must confront the reality of prison not as an interlude in a white middle-class existence but as a stage of the Way re-defining the nature of my life. Prison is then of such duration and intensity that from within the experience I am forced to come to terms with prison as the context of my very life. How free can the choice of prison (through a deliberate act of civil disobedience or a chosen way of life which invites prosecution by the State) remain for me when the severity and duration of my sentence seem to absorb my very life, and instead of feeling myself passing through the role of prisoner I *become* the State's prisoner? What will my sense of freedom be at that point where my principal identity in terms of the institutions of my society is no longer citizen but prisoner?[23]

Church groups encourage an intimacy between Christians; yet intimacy makes it harder to survive in prison. This is why we cannot always express the deep kind of caring community we believe in.

You have to do life somewhere. If I have to do it here, I'll do it here. And if I have to do it here, I'll do it to the best of my ability and I'll try and do it for God . . . for this I need help.

I thought the church was ineffective until a minister went to court with me. . . . We need to see new models of churchmen; the old ones are bad.

The guys think church people have more power than they do. I still think they [the church] should have 10,000 times the commitment I've seen. The Muslims fill the chapel because they give not only rhetoric but try and help in everyday lives. Chaplains suspect a guy's motives; they don't want to be made use of—yet isn't that what chaplains are for? Churches are compassionate but ineffective. They don't deal with anything real. The guys see the church as a crutch, a way to pass the time. I heard a preacher say once, "Christ is a revolutionary," but he didn't do anything about it.

The churches are interested in *morality*; the guys are interested in *legality*. I believe churches are concerned, but they get frustrated, too, and give up. Right now I wish the churches would help us get a bigger visiting room and better food. Churches could also let families know they care what happens to a guy. That would give them [families] courage to speak out. Muslims are united; Christians ought to be.

There is not enough time to deal with problems in the chaplain's office. The men want to feel they are being heard. Groups from churches could do this, especially if they followed it up. Availability is important . . . and especially trust. So many people break trust with us. If you promise something and cannot follow through, tell the man, write it on a piece of toilet paper . . . somehow, let him know you're working on it! So often chapel services are like parading a beautiful banquet before the men, but they come out hungry.

The church has kept the poor complacent through the years. Occasionally a prophet would break through and change things. Jesus was the greatest of the prophets. The church today isn't so bad that it doesn't want to help, but it doesn't help because it doesn't know how. Who will lead the church in this concern? There is no leader! My own church let me down. I was always very active, but no one except my mother comes to see me. I asked the pastor to write a letter to the judge for me . . . he didn't. Nobody cares. I'm disillusioned with the church, but when someone from the church lets me know they care and it's more than just a visit, I'm ready to listen.

Churches are useless because they cannot do anything. When it comes to direct action and sacrifice, churchmen don't act.

We need reality not ritual. We don't want to hear "God moves in a mysterious way" anymore to rationalize why we ought to be content here.

Like the rest of the paid staff, the churches come and go. If you don't have the strength to apply the Scriptures, how can your cries be answered?

I had come to believe that there is no God; if there is, men do not know anything about him. Therefore, all religions were phony—which made all preachers and priests, in our eyes, fakers, including the ones scurrying around the prison . . . men of the cloth who work in prison have an ineradicable stigma attached to them in the eyes of the convicts because they escort condemned men into the gas chamber. Such men of God are powerful arguments in favor of atheism.[24]

## SUMMARY

As we listened, we saw some things we had not seen clearly before. First, we saw that prisoners really were not uniform in background or attitude. Second, we saw how hard it would be for our two hours to make an impression when inserted parenthetically into two hundred hours of contrasting experiences. We also saw the difficulty of dealing with the angry militant who felt that reform, rehabilitation, and any church programs were only methods of manipulating him into an evil system. Often prisoners were saying to the church as well as the prison system, "The hell with you and your system! I'm not going to have any part of it," and often the church has replied as has the prison system, "We don't know how to deal with that kind of bluntness too well."[25] Yet it was also clear that when the church as an institution became identified with personal, Christian love, concern, and action, bridges of credibility and openness to its message were established. As John Erwin at Cook County Jail said, "The way you overcome this disadvantage [the church's credibility] is teaching a man to read . . . one has to earn the right to preach."[26]

We had also learned one more thing. There was a dramatic contrast between the biblical concept of justice noted in the previous chapter and the system of justice that has created the prison system described in this chapter.

**CHAPTER 5**

# Insights into Justice

It is easy for us and others to point out the colossal failure of prisons. However, a more helpful kind of criticism would be that which seeks the root cause of the failure of prisons.

Prisons fail because they fail to provide three crucial marks of biblical justice: *immediacy, relevancy,* and *hope.* At the conclusion of this chapter some biblical illustrations for these marks are given.

## IMMEDIACY

Delayed justice is no justice. Our present penal system and especially the prisons within that system are designed to drag out the process of justice for months and years, even a lifetime. Some say that if a person comes to a speedy trial and receives his or her sentence, then justice has been swift. A speedy trial is equated with justice. This is not so if he or she receives the sentence of a prison term. The complete process of justice includes punishment. If justice delayed is justice denied, then prisons are no part of justice. To have justice, there must be immediacy not only in the trial and judgment but also in the punishment.

There are psychological reasons for this biblical mark of immediacy. It is a well-established behavioral principle that the closer in time a punishment or reward is to an act, the greater its reinforcing power to mold future behavior. A prison term separates the crime from the punishment. A prison term, instead of teaching a person to hate his crime, teaches him to hate the system: administrators, social workers, guards, preachers, and whoever else touches his raw psychological wounds while he is imprisoned. Prisoners can be logically expected not to use time to meditate on their crime, but rather to use time for the purpose of growing in bitterness. The quote of the inmate on the "Today" show in chapter 4 is accurate: "prisons teach persons to do time." Time erases any meaningful connection between what they are suffering and the crime that caused the suffering. Therefore, prisons cannot logically be expected to deter crime. By contrast, the mark of God's justice is a close relation in time between crime and punishment. This will be seen later in this chapter.

## RELEVANCY

If a person kills, he goes to prison. If a person robs, he goes to prison. If a person sells drugs, he goes to prison. There is little relation between the crime a person commits and the kind of punishment he or she receives. Even the number of years a person is imprisoned is so arbitrary that a person convicted for the robbery of $5 may spend more years in prison than one who has embezzled $500,000. "It is criminal to steal a purse; daring to steal a fortune; a mark of greatness to steal a crown. The blame diminishes as the guilt increases." So spoke Schiller of the injustices of the eighteenth century. Justice has not changed much since. This lack of relevancy serves only to embitter persons toward the system.

Most prisoners admit to being guilty of their crimes.[1] Therefore prisoners *do* understand the reason for their punishment. It is the method and inequalities of punishment and not punishment itself that make men and women angry and block any effort at rehabilitation. The anger thus generated by lack of relevancy must be dealt with as a part of any offer of redemptive hope.

It should be noted that some judges and some state codes of justice now provide for relevant sentencing. Minnesota has a new program that allows convicted persons to make restitution in ways *related to their offence*.[2] Other states have such statutes[3] but are slow to implement them. Non-prison sentencing recognizes that there is no way you can "socialize" a prisoner by keeping him or her out of society. One inmate put it this way, "If you put a dog in a cage and kick it once a day for five years then say, 'O.K., I hope you've learned your lesson,' no wonder he bites you on the knee when he gets out!" Prison terms that remove a person from society are self-defeating if the purpose of our penal system is to place responsible persons back into the stream of society.

It is not my purpose to list types of relevant punishment here but rather to point out that prisons do not meet this requirement of justice and that churches seeking a redemptive role must understand the anger this lack of relevancy generates. By contrast, the mark of God's justice is a relevant relationship between crime and punishment. This, too, will be seen later in this chapter.

## HOPE

One might think that the only sentences that would deprive a person of hope are "life imprisonment" or "death." But hope is destroyed by any prison term that keeps a person one day beyond the point where he or she feels worthless as a human being. Hope could be destroyed in serving a sentence of a few months if a person did not have the inner resources to tolerate the degrading atmosphere of a prison for more than a few weeks. This loss of hope would not be the result of a purposeful design by administrators, nor would this loss of hope necessarily be due to long sentences. It would be due to forces that shape the prisoner long before he or she reaches prison and which are accentuated in a prison system supported by a public that wants to forget the prisoner; that wants to "lock the door and throw the key away." As long as the public wants that kind of prison, administrators will have little ability to make their institutions anything but hopeless. While anger at a lack of relevancy makes a redemptive role difficult, this lack of hope makes it impossible. I believe that no person changes unless he or she has hope. God's model of justice as described in the following section of this chapter not only provides a close relation between crime and punishment in time and kind, but it also leaves a person with hope.

## SOME BIBLICAL CASES

In exploring the Scriptures one is struck by the fact that the idea of prisons is found nowhere in the biblical system of justice. In the Scriptures sin is always punished, but imprisonment is never the means. The Christian church must take much of the credit or blame for our "modern" prisons. A part of the history of prisons is the establishment by the churches of places of penance (thus the word "penitentiary"). In an earlier day it was thought that giving a person some quiet in which to think, separating one from the distractions of society and exposing one to the Bible would bring about repentance and change. Like so many systems, we kept it going long after it was obvious that it did not work.[4]

The modern prisoner seldom knows where he or she stands in the complex process between conviction and release. An inmate is always in a "never-never land" full of forms, bureaucracy, favoritism, and chance. This cruel uncertainty is never present in God's justice. In the Scripture, justice had these threefold characteristics of immediacy, relevancy, and hope. To illustrate this, I have chosen three cases from Scripture. There are others that could have been selected, but these have been chosen because they show God's dealings with a cross section of society—a king, an adulteress, and a church member.

King David was one of God's favorite persons. In 2 Samuel, chapter 11, there is the account of David's double sin of adultery and murder. Immediately, as recorded in chapter 12, the prophet Nathan was sent to David to issue God's sentence. The child born of adultery and sired by a murderer would die. As hard as this sentence was, David was able to cope with it; for, first, he immediately knew where he stood with God; second, he knew it was an all-too relevant sentence; and third, he soon was given evidence that God had not abandoned him—that there was hope. A second child, Solomon, was born as a token of God's forgiveness and hope for the future. "And the Lord loved him, and sent a message by Nathan the prophet" (2 Samuel 12:24-25). The same prophet who had pronounced sentence offered hope. God showed justice to his beloved David with immediacy, relevancy, and hope.

Adulteresses would hardly seem in the same social class with kings, but God's justice bears the same marks for all. We see this in the case of the adulteress dragged before Jesus for his judgment (John 8:1-11).[5] The Law of Moses said that she should be killed (Leviticus 20:10). But as Jesus interpreted the law, he saw the need for relevancy and hope as well as the immediacy indicated by this law. Jesus let the shame of her exposure serve as her judgment; it was immediate and relevant to her crime. He also gave a sentence to her jury of accusers and reinforced the idea that only God, who is sinless, can give the sentence of death. Finally, in her brokenness

Jesus gave her hope, not excusing her but redeeming her. He freed her for a new beginning as he said, "Neither do I condemn you; go, and do not sin again" (John 8:11). Jesus carried out God's justice with immediacy, relevancy, and hope.

One final case, that of a church member. It is one thing for God's prophet to be the instrument of God's justice, or for the Son of God to be his messenger, but can a local congregation be entrusted with the carrying out of justice? Paul was committed to the fact that it could. "Do you not know that we are to judge angels? How much more matters pertaining to this life?" (1 Corinthians 6:3). As the early church under Paul's influence struggled with the matter of justice and sought God's guidance, they too discovered the principles of immediacy, relevancy, and hope. This is illustrated in the case of the church member who had sexual relations with his stepmother (1 Corinthians 5:1-5). Paul rebuked the church for delaying their sentencing and immediately issued his own. The man should be cast away from the church fellowship. He would now lose the fellowship of the people whom he had hurt by his conduct. Justice was immediate and relevant. But there was hope. Paul says the purpose of this discipline is that "his spirit may be saved in the day of the Lord Jesus" (1 Corinthians 5:5). In a later letter Paul, realizing the sentence has been carried out, apparently with the result of repentance and a change of behavior, writes: "For such a one this punishment by the majority is enough; so you should rather turn to forgive and comfort him, or he may be overwhelmed by excessive sorrow. So I beg you to reaffirm your love for him" (2 Corinthians 2:6-8).

Again we see the principles of immediacy, relevancy, and hope.

This model of justice can be seen throughout the Scriptures. In proportion to our departure from these three principles, our penal systems will fail and the church's mission will be made more difficult.

## WHY WE FAIL TO EXCHANGE MODELS

I believe we have failed to accept God's model of justice because of our uncertainty. We are not confident judges. In every criminal we see a little of ourselves. We know our own complicated motives and realize how little we know about the motives of the fellow human we are to judge. God knows the heart; we do not.

Our humanness is our weakness, and this leaves us in a vulnerable position as judges.

"Progress" and "civilization" seem only to have made the distance between God's model of justice and human penal systems greater. Even in the pre-Christian codes of the Mosaic Law justice was swift and was related directly to the crime. Simple or primitive societies have neither the time nor resources for prisons, and people are close enough to one another to have some confidence in judgment. The early Hebrew society came closer to the swiftness and creativity of God's justice than our later more "highly developed" systems of justice.

The issue of capital punishment is a dramatization of our present dilemma. The public seems to want the death sentence on the books; yet when the public finds itself on juries, it is reluctant to bring the verdicts that carry mandatory executions. It appears that we are too fearful to be merciful and not sure enough of ourselves to kill. Prisons are our "cop-out." There we can punish without killing, but we certainly don't rehabilitate, much less offer redemptive hope. Our uncertainty, due to the walls built up between human beings, makes it difficult for us to dare to try a new model of justice.

God, who knows the human heart altogether, has no such uncertainty—"He looses the fateful lightning of His terrible swift sword!" Because God is a confident judge, he can also be a merciful judge. With the swiftness of God's justice there is also hope, focused perfectly in the message of Jesus Christ.

The church of Jesus Christ must work to bring in God's model of justice: a system where there is immediacy, relevancy, and hope. A legitimate part of our mission is to work for the political and institutional changes that will move our society toward that end. However, we cannot wait for such change to come before ministering to and through the system as it is. The insights of this chapter helped our group to understand some of the contradictions of the present system of justice and the frustrations they create. Such understanding is necessary for a realistic and helpful ministry in today's prisons.

### CHAPTER 6

# Beginning Again

This book seems to have wandered far since the reality of Jim and Mike and others forced us to search for surer foundations and clearer directions. Yet the previous three chapters were necessary "homework" for us and for any who dare to undertake a prison ministry. Understanding the message of the Scriptures, the experience of prison, and the contradictions of justice should have been where we began. Yet perhaps we took what we learned more to heart because we were driven to it by failure.

I would like to report that after doing this "homework" every problem was solved and every effort was crowned with success. Obviously not. But we did more fully understand some of the forces that shaped us, both inmate and outmate. We did find the deliverance from despair that comes when one experiences the call to obey instead of a call to succeed. We did realize that signs of redemption might be few and that we might not even recognize them when they occurred.

## SIGNS OF REDEMPTION

Yet as we continued our ministry beyond the first year, we did see signs that were recognizable to us. Some of these might seem insignificant to an outsider; yet to us in the prison atmosphere, permeated with failure, they seemed very bright.

### Clark

One of these events involved Clark. It occurred during a time when some of us were sharing our past history. Clark told us he was in jail for a check-cashing scheme, a "con game." Then he began to share experience after experience relating the various ways he had conned people all his life. Articulate and clever, Clark held our attention for over an hour. "And how do you know I'm not conning you now?" he suddenly asked. Before any of us could respond, he said, "How I wish I could level with people . . . the only hope I have is in this group."

Following this, there was a chorus of voices from inmates and outmates trying to support Clark in his anguish, aware that Clark had shared an honest feeling for the first time in a long while. We did not always have spoken prayers in the group, but that evening we gathered together shoulder-to-shoulder to offer our prayers that Clark would find deliverance from the need to deceive others and himself. Recently, as Clark neared the end of his term, he made the anguished statement, "I'm either going to leave this prison a changed man or a criminal!" He knew these were the only alternatives. For a person like Clark to acknowledge the possibility of failure and share his struggle with us was a sign of redemption.

### Ben

Ben had been a part of our group for over a year before we really heard from him. His manner indicated that he was often agitated within; yet he seldom spoke. We asked ourselves, "Why did he come; what was bugging him?" Ben's secret did not come out until we had begun to divide the larger group into groups of four. Somehow in that setting Ben felt he could unload his feelings, and he did. He told us of enduring the hate of a whole city after being accused of complicity in the murder of a policeman. He felt he had a legitimate case for a retrial, but he could get absolutely no action. He was in the group hoping someone might "go to bat" for him. I wondered why Ben had waited over a year to cry for help. As he talked, we realized that in the presence of any group or authority figure he became tongue-tied. Confronted by even a single official, he could not express himself. Meeting with sixteen "friends" in the group was still too much. But the smaller group of four of us made it possible for Ben to speak. He poured out his troubles and burdens. We were not able to do too much about his legal needs, but Ben did find more and more confidence in speaking for himself, first in the group of sixteen and then before prison officials. As of this writing, he hopes to obtain a new trial within a few months, mainly due to a courage and confidence he began to discover in a very small group of people willing to listen.

## Sonny

Sonny had been in and out of prisons since he was a young teenager. Even with his hard life, Sonny, who was in his forties, looked under thirty. Sonny was a talker and attempted to con when he thought it would accomplish his purposes. Before he came to our group, Sonny had participated in a Yokefellow Group in another prison. This experience had taken some of the artificial polish off of Sonny, and he had begun to acknowledge that he didn't have all the answers. Our group tried to help Sonny continue this personal growth by letting him know that it was okay to depend on others, that we need each other.

Sonny finally reached the time for his release. We expressed our concern before he left as to whether the old Sonny who wanted to appear polished, self-sufficient, and too smart to lose again would leave, or the new Sonny who was learning he needed other people for strength. We got part of our answer on the last night he was with us when he said, "I wish you would pray for me; it's not going to be easy." Everybody did, even some in the group who had never prayed aloud before.

## John

John was one of the least "religious" persons in our group. He had not rejected religion; it simply had never been a part of his experience outside prison. John said he lived by what he called his "code of honor." This meant to him it was okay to steal but not okay to hurt people physically. He said that he hated "stool pigeons," hypocrites, and the rich. He held a hatred of rapists and murderers that exceeded that of most "law-abiding" citizens. However, John himself had been convicted of over a dozen crimes.

As John learned to trust the group, he began to share his past history. He revealed a life of very few warm, family relationships. We could begin to see the reasons for his inconsistent standards and bitterness. The only person from his family who currently had any relationship with him was a sister. He said that he hated her because he felt that she had "let him down" in the past. During one meeting we discussed the power of bitterness and how this emotion could twist and destroy our lives. John challenged us many times as we talked about the power of forgiveness in freeing us from bitterness. He just couldn't see forgiving anyone who had hurt him; God might be able to forgive, but not he. Phil, an older inmate in the group, remembering his own long years of bitterness reinforced what we were sharing with John. About four weeks later John came into our meeting and said, "Hey, I've got to tell you something. . . ." He told us about receiving a letter from his sister and said that this time he had answered it. She had then written back a gracious letter and had asked to visit him. (Until that time he had refused to see her.) Some weeks after this John told us about the visit itself and the reconciliation that had taken place. John had never before been so excited. His whole manner changed that night from that of a sullen, angry man to a child who was discovering that there was healing joy in forgiveness.

### Jake

Jake was a lifer. He was in prison on the basis of the testimony of a woman who had been hurt by Jake's crime many years ago. Jake had been in prison so long and was so respected there that he had been recommended for a pardon. Every year for the last few years, Jake's case had been reviewed by the Board of Pardons. Every year that woman would be present to tell the Board how she feared for her life should Jake ever be pardoned. Every year Jake failed to get his pardon. Jake was able to share this story with the group a number of times, and each time his anger at this woman seemed to diminish and his understanding of her experience seemed greater. The group tried to help Jake to see that this woman was in a prison of fear as destructive as the prison of stone in which he lived. Jake finally reached the point where he was able to deal with this woman not in bitterness but in pity. This step of forgiveness gave Jake a new calm as the yearly review of his case approached. Perhaps the Board was tiring of hearing about this woman's fears, or it is possible that Jake's new maturity regarding this woman was noted by his caseworker in his report to the Board. At any rate, this time Jake received his pardon. Whatever the reason, he had an opportunity to begin again.

## Dan

Dan had been on "death row." Although his sentence had been commuted to life imprisonment, Dan's experience on death row had left deep marks on his attitude. He said that he often asked himself, "Why have I been spared?" and "Who controls life and death?" He had the idea that life was out of his control; that he was a puppet in the hands of the state and, ultimately, in the hands of God. This feeling left Dan with a sense of powerlessness. He said that he was a Christian; but as he talked, we discovered that the God he served left him no freedom or redemptive power. One week we talked about the subject "Can You Die Before Your Time?" (suggested by Dan). The group studied Luke 12:4-7 where Jesus speaks about the hairs of our head being numbered and about our great value in God's sight. We discussed how God's knowledge of us, and love for us, does not take away our freedom to accept or reject his guidance. An outmate in the group shared her experience of redemptive release when she first realized that God loved her enough to let her risk making choices with her life. Another person shared his belief about the meaning of Genesis 1:26: "Let us make man in our own image"—that this means we have the God-like privilege of choosing our destiny. The idea that he was *not* a victim of inevitable circumstances beyond his control so excited Dan that he grabbed my arm when we returned two weeks later and said, "What happened at our last meeting really changed me; life is a whole new ball game for me." With some hope restored, Dan is making plans for his future and taking action on them, realizing that God will not do for him what he can do for himself. This has resulted in his first furlough and a job opportunity in a Christian camping program for troubled youth.

## Jeff

Jeff came to the group a hopeless man. He was serving thirty to sixty years. He had already served seventeen years and in that time had lost his wife through divorce and his children through lack of contact. To the best of his knowledge he had neither family nor friend. Our group was literally Jeff's last hope. In the group Jeff's progress was slow; but as we tried to show that we cared about him, he began to feel there was a purpose in living. He asked his counselor to apply for a commutation of his sentence, a step he had felt hopeless about before. Some of us wrote letters on his behalf. His sentence was finally commuted to twenty to forty years. This still seemed like "forever" to us outmates, but it put Jeff within three years of release and put some prerelease programs within his reach. I do not believe that it was just these legal changes that gave Jeff his basic hope, but rather the continuing encouragement of the group. God was reminding Jeff through people who cared that even though there were years to wait and even though there was no one waiting for him, he was important to God. Jeff finally had his first furlough with one of our church families and, while he was out, he discovered an elderly aunt who still remembered him. How important that was to him! Hope is replacing despair as he talks in terms of what he will do when his long wait is over.

### An Outmate

Signs of redemption were not only seen in inmates. One outmate who was going through severe family problems also found her own faith strengthened and hope renewed in the group. As she saw men like Jeff recover hope, she began to believe all was not lost in her case. Gradually she began to take an interest in some of the inmates by writing them and visiting them. They in turn encouraged her. This experience was one of many whereby inmates ministered to outmates with their own insights about God.

## MEETING BASIC NEEDS

A pattern was becoming clearer through these experiences. Though inmates represent all the variety of personalities found on the outside, there were two characteristics that seemed preeminent among our inmate friends. The personal experiences in this chapter reveal them. The first is a difficulty in facing reality, and the second is a low estimation of self-worth.

Prisons, because they remove a person from customary social contacts, encourage fantasizing. This loss of touch with reality is a natural reaction to the deprivation of social contacts and the accompanying sensory deprivation that occurs in prisons. This unreal environment affects an inmate's ability to know himself since most self-knowledge comes as a result of the response we get from other persons. Self-understandings that would seem natural and obvious outside prison walls become significant signs of growth among inmates. [1]

We found that one of the most effective ways to help an inmate face reality about himself was for an outmate to do it first. It was essential for outmates to model an openness of expression first before expecting it of inmates since inmates had so much more to lose. Inmates were taking a great risk if they told us what they felt about themselves. They all knew cases where such material had been used against fellow-inmates by lawyers, psychologists, and even chaplains. In keeping trust and in modeling our own openness, we tried to make it easier for inmates to face reality about themselves. This problem of being open was complicated further because inmates are usually rewarded for controlling their feelings, not expressing them. In effect we were inviting men to share their feelings, even their hostilities, knowing that after the meeting was over, the system would demand that these feelings be bottled up again. We believed that this risk was worth taking since these feelings might come out at a more dangerous time if not expressed in the group and that no redemptive progress was possible without this facing of reality.

As regards self-worth, we found that a low estimation of self-worth was a prevalent characteristic of inmates. This is not immediately apparent because it is covered over by many words and mannerisms. As most of us shared our backgrounds, it became clear that inmates had experienced failure in almost every arena of growing up. They learned to feel "I'm not OK—You're OK" [2] in relationships with parents, teachers, and peers.

The failure of family relationships was the most obvious cause. Few inmates recalled a secure family life. Current insights of sociology and psychology reveal the importance of family roots and traditions in healthy human and social development. Yet these men, mainly from displaced minority groups, had very few family roots and were often cut off from any sense of traditions. Paul writes a perfect description of prisoners as he speaks of the Gentiles in Ephesians 2:12 (TEV): "You were foreigners, and did not belong to God's chosen people. You had no part in the covenants, which were based on God's promises to his people. You lived in this world without hope and without God."

We began to realize how important it was to help these men

restore whatever family ties they had left (often very few) as a part of their recovery of self-worth. We realized that we were fighting huge odds in throwing our feeble weights against the massive wall of their "Not OK" feelings. Yet, we knew from our own experience that accepting one's worth before God and others was a crucial part of redemption. The experiences of this chapter reflect both the difficulty and the desire to communicate this self-worth. We observed a further important consequence when a feeling of self-worth was recovered. We saw that only when a participant had a secure feeling about his or her own worth could he or she be free to care about others.

## DISCOVERING NEW MINISTRIES

As the group slowly and haltingly began to remove the need for self-justification (conning) and replace it with self-worth, participants, both inmates and outmates, became free to look around and see human needs they had not seen before. A willingness to inconvenience and even jeopardize oneself for the good of another is the final test of redemptive change. It is the example set by Jesus Christ. There were some incidents that revealed such growth.

### Tom and Mr. W

Tom was an older inmate who was an alcoholic. He also had cancer, and the prognosis was that he would not live much longer. Tom was not an appealing person either in looks or personality. As we met together, I observed that one of the outmates, Mr. W, paid special attention to Tom. He had a unique way of helping Tom express himself and of challenging Tom without offending him. This outmate seemed to be able to read Tom's mind. I learned that this outmate had been an alcoholic, too, but had recovered through AA and the efforts of another group of caring Christians. He had walked in Tom's shoes, and therefore to an extent he *did* know how Tom thought. No one could have helped Tom in the way this outmate did. He not only was sensitive to Tom, but also he represented hope to Tom. He was a believable proof that Tom could live a life free from alcohol. Ex-addicts of any kind and ex-inmates who have found redemptive freedom are great assets to any group, because they can empathize without being manipulated.

Furthermore, such people are living proof that there is hope!

## Jake and Mr. J

One of the outmates, Mr. J, took a special interest in Jake (whose case was mentioned earlier). He saw Jake's growing maturity in forgiving his old foe and realized the esteem in which Jake was held among the inmates. This outmate decided he would do all he could to make sure Jake got his pardon the next time he went before the Board of Pardons. He talked with Jake outside our group sessions; he wrote letters; and he tried to see what he could do about the woman who seemed to stand between Jake and freedom. He personally attended the Board's meetings. I believe that the added personal interest of this outmate in addition to Jake's growth in understanding spelled the difference between failure and success in gaining Jake's pardon.

## Dan and Mrs. W and Mrs. R

Dan, who found new hope for his life, still held a life sentence. Two outmates, Mrs. W and Mrs. R, volunteered to go on his behalf to the hearing which would consider giving Dan a specific sentence instead of life imprisonment. This would be the only way any of Dan's future could ever occur outside the walls. At such hearings the prisoner is not heard, only those who will speak for or against him. For the two women to do this meant a long trip to Philadelphia, a long wait while many cases were heard, and standing up before five persons (one of whom was the lieutenant governor) to make a speech. I don't believe there is any way these women would have done this previously. It was a sign of God's redemptive power that they were willing and able to do this. The only affirmations with any religious dimension that day came from a Black Muslim leader who testified for another inmate and from these two outmates who testified how Dan had found hope for a new life through God's redemptive love.

## John and Tom

Inmates also took risks for other inmates in the group. John, realizing that Tom was in need of treatment for his cancer, saw to it that he either got to the infirmary or that he got the proper medicine in his cell. John did for Tom what the administration and outmates could not or would not do. He made Tom's days easier by sticking close by and being available when needed. Even the guards did not interfere with John if he was on an errand of mercy for Tom. Partly because John saw to it that Tom got the care he needed, he recovered enough to leave the prison.

## EXTENDING THE MINISTRY

The inmate participants were acutely aware that many men who needed what the group offered could not be included. They spoke to the chaplain about expanding what we had begun. At their insistence and with the chaplain's encouragement four or five other groups gradually came into being. Some of these utilized outmates from other churches who had spent some time meeting with our group. Other church-related persons were drawn into this ministry. Most groups affiliated with Yokefellows in some way as our original group had done. All had Christian roots, but each one was unique, depending on the skills, gifts, and needs of inmates and outmates.

Initially, there was great doubt in the minds of the prison administration and inmates as to whether a church located in a white, close-knit, suburban community could relate to poor, ghetto blacks who made up the majority of the prison population. (This is not to imply that such persons commit most crimes, only that such persons are given jail terms.) I believe that our experiences demonstrated that we were able to relate in some significant ways even though most of our inmate friends were from the black communities of Philadelphia. The Reverend David Meyers, an institutional chaplain in the Philadelphia area who has initiated Yokefellow Prison Groups there, said, "We cannot provide exposure to the community they came from or will return to; all we can provide is love."[3] This statement clarifies what we can and cannot do.

I would also add that two of the inmates in the group, having no family left in the Philadelphia area, are making tentative plans to reside in our area upon release. Resettling these men in our area will be a further challenge to us.

Our efforts were not aimed at providing job skills, nor were we able to move the administration in developing this area of need. We have a growing feeling that this is a serious deficiency. The M-2

Job Therapy and PACE programs described in Appendix A demonstrate the importance of job skills in achieving self-worth and in experiencing redemptive change. In our future plans we hope that we can deal with this area of need.

## EPILOGUE

Many evenings we returned from the prison emotionally drained. This was primarily due to the fact that we had experienced a tiny bit of the hopelessness that the inmates experience—a hopelessness due to personal problems that often began at birth, family problems that had been building for years, and legal problems that were so complex that they defied understanding. It took a great effort to lift the hopes of the inmates by our words and actions instead of being dragged down into this hopelessness ourselves. Some evenings we felt victorious in this effort, and some we did not. Yet, the fact that both inmates and outmates continued to minister to one another indicated that God's redemptive grace was at work. We did not reform the penal system or even transform a prison of 1,600 men. We had made serious mistakes in what we had attempted, but God was making a positive and, we trust, a lasting impact on the lives of a couple dozen inmates and outmates. Even our frustration at dealing with such a small number of people was being overcome as we saw other groups being established. Our hope is that this book will encourage other churches and Christians to dare to begin their own prison ministry. The next chapter suggests some "Ways You Can Begin." It comes out of our mistakes and joys in over five years of ministry.

### CHAPTER 7

# Ways You Can Begin

As I think about it, this book really is an "institutional altar call": a call for the institutional church to minister in such a way that Christ can say, "I was in prison and you came to me" (Matthew 25:36). It seems clear to me that if churches as well as individuals do not hear and respond to this call, the job will not be done.

This chapter will give professional and lay church persons some guidelines for action. It uses the insights gained by our church and others. This chapter goes beyond an "institutional altar call"; it describes what a church can do after it has responded to the call.

First, a set of *action* steps that can be taken as a church prepares for a prison ministry is given. In these steps reference will be made to material where specific help can be found. Then, a set of *attitudes* that should permeate these action steps is described. Following this, an orientation/training program for participants in a prison ministry is suggested. A concluding section will give additional guidelines to local churches that wish to use a small group model similar to the one our church used. There is a final paragraph on "expectations."

When the word "church" is used in this chapter, the phrase "cluster of churches" can be substituted. A cluster of churches is a more permanent base on which to build a prison ministry, and this approach should be encouraged whenever possible.

## GUIDELINES FOR ACTION

The following set of steps can lead to effective action. The steps are written for a professional or lay church person willing to initiate them.

### Step 1

Examine your own biblical and theological assumptions about prisons and a prison ministry. Determine the biblical and theological assumptions of your congregation. In light of these assumptions find a forum to share your own insights. Chapter 3 of this book suggests some biblical references for study. The following books can be used for help in stimulating theological reflection, *The Crime of Punishment, Justice and the Imprisoned, The Fire in Today's Prisons, Return to the World, ". . . And the Criminals with Him.*[1] A series of sermons or midweek programs could be used to provide a biblical and theological base and motivation for a prison ministry.

### Step 2

Discover the needs and opportunities around you. Find out where the prisons (penitentiaries, jails, etc.) are located. Find out if there are ex-inmates in your community and what their needs are. Find out if there are prison staff in your community (or in your church) and what needs they see. Arrange to have lunch with the prison chaplain. Through him you may want to arrange a meeting with the superintendent of the prison. Invite these and other prison personnel to share their insights with the congregation. There are usually ex-inmates available who can articulate needs for a congregation. For clarifying your understanding of prisons the following books are recommended: *Inside Prison American Style, Letters from Attica, Soledad Brother: The Prison Letters of George Jackson, Asylums, Ministering to Prisoners and Their Families,* and *Kind and Usual Punishment: The Prison Business.*[2]

### Step 3

Bring together a "task force" of people who will work with you and represent the total church in developing a prison ministry. There are a number of ways in which this can be done. As information is shared through the programs described in Step 2, some persons will readily express their interest. Further interest can be determined by circulating an "interest finder" among the congregation. A sermon on the need for prison ministries could be followed by an opportunity for people to respond. In these ways a task force can be formed. It would provide important insights for the task force to have as a member someone from the church who was an ex-offender or at least had come through an experience of failure and forgiveness.

At some point this task force should be officially recognized by the total church. If a pastor has initiated this concern, he or she may wish to find a lay person competent and concerned enough to be the coordinator for this group and delegate future responsibilities to that person. The task force will work closely with the pastor or coordinator in the following steps.

## Step 4

Find out what others have done. This book and the projects noted in Appendix A will give some ideas. There is a great deal of material available at the addresses given and most of it is free. Yokefellows International, mentioned in Appendix A, can put you in touch with local chapters that often publish their own material. Yokefellow of Pennsylvania has been especially helpful to us. To keep abreast of current events, review some or all of the following periodicals: *Fortune News, Release, VIP* [Volunteers in Probation] *Examiner,* or *Crime and Delinquency.*[3] Share this material with the task force so they can see the great variety of possible ministries.

## Step 5

Establish your purpose(s). (Purposes describe long-range ideals and an overall vision for the project. Goals are more specific, shorter in range, and provide more concrete proposals against which to evaluate the project. See Step 7 for the setting of goals.) Given your biblical/theological assumptions and the needs as you see them, develop some purposes for a prison ministry. The purposes established for our ministry are listed in chapter 1 and illustrate what fitted our situation.

The purposes which the task force develops should be shared with the congregation and revised if necessary. The congregation should have some way of voting for or affirming these purposes as representing the thinking of the church as a whole and not just of the task force. There should be a continuing effort to keep the congregation informed and supportive. In some close-knit communities it will also be necessary to help the community understand these purposes. This can be done through open church meetings, newspaper releases, and by speaking to local civic groups.

## Step 6

Define the scope of your ministry. No church, unless it is a large church, can deal with all aspects of our present system of justice. Some churches will wish to work on the causes of criminal behavior, others with released prisoners, still others with penal reform. This book deals mainly with a ministry within prison walls. Defining the scope helps a church focus its energies where it seems best suited to minister.

## Step 7

Keeping in mind the difference between purposes and goals (see Step 5), set goals that are achievable within a specific length of time and, as much as possible, are measurable. These goals should be realistic enough to gain the support of the church but ambitious enough to be worthy of your efforts. Sample goals would be: "Provide a one-year training program in auto repair for ten inmates," or "Set up a task force for interracial contacts between six members of the congregation and six inmates; to include home visits, worship experiences, and prison meetings." Since your purpose must include meeting the needs of inmates, their participation in setting goals is important. If the goals require the expenditure of funds, plans should be made for raising those funds. A broad base of support extending beyond a single church is helpful in funding.

## Step 8

Select methods that suit the purposes and goals you have selected and that suit the resources your church and its task force have to offer. Many methods are used in the projects mentioned in the Appendix.

A number of additional models for prison ministries may be

found in *Fire in Today's Prisons.*[4] Rapport between the task force and the prison chaplain and/or superintendent should be such that permission can be asked and given for the method/model you have selected. If permission is not granted, methods and scope will have to be renegotiated until they are mutually acceptable.

## Step 9

Plan and conduct an orientation/training program. A suggested orientation/training program is given later in this chapter.

## Step 10

Begin your program. Deciding when to begin is crucial. If you begin too soon, without adequate preparation, you invite mistakes. In most of our church programs we can make a serious mistake, fail, and try again. Within prison walls there are few second chances. You are always on trial before administration and inmates, and serious mistakes may not be tolerated.

On the other hand, if you wait too long to begin, the vision loses momentum and people forget the imperatives that first stirred their concern. Concern is kept alive as people participate in the project.

About six months would be a reasonable time for this ten-step process.

## Step 11

Make periodic evaluations. In order to make and keep the ministry effective, results must be measured against both purposes and goals. As mentioned in Step 7, a good goal contains measurable criteria. In prison ministries these criteria are often hard to measure, but over a period of two or three months the group usually gains enough information to begin to evaluate effectively. The chaplain and, whenever possible, the inmates should be invited to share in these meetings.

## GUIDELINES FOR ATTITUDES

The following "Seven Commandments" should serve as guidelines for prison work. They are crucial attitudes for a church that is committed to a redemptive style of ministry.

## Commandment 1

*Recognize that the administrative and security personnel of the prison, as well as the inmates, face severe problems and need redemptive change.* A prison ministry that is not sensitive to the total needs of the prison is not a complete ministry and will not be as helpful to the inmates. This includes a willingness to obey (though not necessarily to agree with) all prison rules.

## Commandment 2

*Keep all the information that is shared as a confidential trust.* Unless you have information which, if not shared, would jeopardize the life or welfare of another person, it should be considered "privileged information" and should be so respected by the prison administration. It takes a long time to build a relationship of trust in a prison, and it can be destroyed by one careless conversation. Information an outmate may have learned in a personal conversation with an inmate should not even be shared with the rest of the group without his or her permission.

## Commandment 3

*Make only those commitments and promises that you are both able and willing to keep.* Within a prison, hope and expectations take on extreme importance. One must be careful never to raise hopes or expectations that cannot be fulfilled. The quote of the inmate in chapter 4 is applicable here:

> If you promise something and can't follow through, tell the man, write it on a piece of toilet paper . . . somehow let him know you're working on it.

One of the outmates made a similar observation:

> When you can't follow through, the inmates lose trust in you; they become disillusioned with another outside program; you break faith with the institution you represent; and you hurt your own integrity.

## Commandment 4

*Insist on honesty from yourself and from others.* To allow any deception or conning to go unchallenged is good for no one. Naiveté is no virtue in prisons. Inmates do tend to manipulate; this often is the only way they know how to survive as individuals. One should understand this problem, but not yield to it. In a redemptive prison ministry, honesty is the only policy: "the truth, the whole truth and nothing but the truth," but the truth with love. (See Ephesians 4:15.) This style must begin with the outmate.

### Commandment 5

*Do not be patronizing.* Christians represent a way of grace, where no one can look down on another. Inmates usually have much to offer outmates and may have a prophetic word for them. Accept the fact that one can both learn from and be ministered to by inmates.

### Commandment 6

*Do not hesitate to share your personal religious faith.* Do not pretend more than you believe or share less than you believe. This is a part of honesty. Most inmates are hungry to hear a word of authentic personal Christian experience. It is the greatest truth we have to share and the heart of our redemptive role.

### Commandment 7

*This ministry is not for kicks but for keeps.* Don't begin it if you only want to see what prisons are like or to have a new kind of experience. Begin it only if you want to get involved for a long time. Inmates have seen enough of "here today, gone tomorrow" religious services and programs. They want, need, and have a right to expect a long-term commitment from Christians.

## A SUGGESTED ORIENTATION/TRAINING PROGRAM

It is important that those who will be ministering in a prison setting participate in an orientation/training program. The following schedule of programs is one way of implementing Step 9 in the *Guidelines for Action* section of this chapter.

This program schedule has five parts. Each part includes a varied number of meetings or sessions. Sessions should last about 1½ hours and provide time for questions and discussion. The prison chaplain should attend as many sessions as possible.

### Part I (one session)

This should be led by the pastor or church coordinator.

1.  Review the steps that brought the group or task force to this point so as to provide each person with a common understanding of the background of this project.
2.  Refocus attention on the biblical and theological understandings that motivate your ministry.
3.  Present the purposes and goals and provide an opportunity for each person to "own" these purposes and goals for themselves through discussion, clarification, and, if necessary, change.
4.  Describe the future sessions in this orientation/training schedule and explain their purpose.

## Part II (two to six sessions)

These sessions should be led by the person(s) who is going to do the training in the method of ministry the church has selected. The nature of these sessions will depend on the method/model selected. For instance, if Transactional Analysis[5] is going to be a tool used in your ministry, a four- to six-week program with a trainer might be necessary. (A tool like Transactional Analysis should not be overtly used in prison sessions unless the inmates have been a part of the training and understand the vocabulary.) If methods such as those used by Yokefellow or M-2 (see Appendix A for more information) are going to be used, then two to four sessions might be required with representatives of these groups leading the training and with the materials to be used on hand. No matter which method is selected, there should be some training in interpersonal relationships that will give a basis for the evaluation that follows Part III.

## Part III (one session)

This would be led by the pastor or church coordinator. Persons from another church or churches who have been involved in a prison ministry would be invited to this session. In this way the group would be able to share with and question those with firsthand experience.

## Evaluation

Before Part IV, the pastor and/or church coordinator will need to make an evaluation of those planning to participate in your ministry. If the chaplain has been a part of this Orientation/Training Program, he should be consulted in this evaluation. This evaluation will decide who will share in your ministry. Since some individuals, because of their own special needs, could jeopardize the program, this is a necessary step. It may be helpful to hold an extra session where those in the group can provide some evaluation of themselves. The criteria for evaluation will depend on the type of ministry selected. Obviously a ministry involving help with vocational skills requires a different kind of person than one involving help with psychological growth.

## Part IV (one or two sessions)

This session should be held at the prison with the chaplain and/or the superintendent in charge. It would be helpful if the superintendent would give an overview of past and present prison policy and his expectations regarding the church's ministry. If possible, someone from the security staff should explain the regulations under which the group will have to operate. The chaplain (who will usually be the liaison person between the church and the prison) should share his vision for the ministry.

A tour of the prison is helpful, not to gape, but to get a feel for the environment and programs that make up the inmate's world.

## Part V

This is a transitional step before beginning your ministry. The church persons involved should meet with the inmates who will be participating in order to discuss purposes, methods, and goals. There should be opportunity for feedback from the inmates and, if necessary, a reformulation of goals before the ministry begins.

### ADDITIONAL GUIDELINES FOR CHURCHES USING A SMALL-GROUP MODEL

For churches that wish to pattern their ministry after our small-group model, the following additional guidelines are suggested.

### Group Size

The size of the group is crucial in developing a deep level of communication. A combined group of twelve inmates and outmates is an effective size for a prison ministry. A flexible format where the larger group of twelve can separate into groups of four or two when needed is best. For more persons, additional groups should be formed. While a 50-50 distribution of inmates and outmates was used in our ministry, the percentage of outmates could be less than 50 percent. This will not provide for as much personal contact but would spread outmate resources further.

## Group Continuity

Personal growth depends on the continuity of participation in such groups. Levels of trust and honesty will take longer to develop in a prison setting than on the outside. The significant breakthroughs in our ministry involved those who were faithful in attendance.

## Group Commitment

Outmates with an informed and deep Christian commitment do not quit easily. Christians who have experienced the gracious love of God themselves are better able to show grace when faced with difficulties and hostilities. It is this experience of grace rather than church membership that gives people staying power in this difficult work.

## Group Action

There must be an action dimension to this type of group no matter how "spiritual" its goals are. Actions always speak louder than words. Only as inmates see outmates writing letters, talking to their families, bringing them books, and contacting judges will they begin to believe their professed concern. This is a two-way street. Outmates should expect inmates to do more than verbalize their insights wherever this is possible for them.

## EXPECTATIONS

One must have realistic expectations if one is not to become discouraged with a prison ministry. Not everyone can be or wants to be helped. The penal system and efforts at rehabilitation in this country have been a colossal failure. Any movement of this stone of hopelessness is a victory. The concluding chapter will emphasize the crucial role of the church in the restoration of hope.

### CHAPTER 8

# Hope: The Way It Can Be

The clearest insight that I have received from our experience is the absolute necessity of hope in experiencing redemptive change. Romans 8:24 states, "For we are saved by hope" (KJV). The sense of this passage is, "If we have no hope, what is the sense of trying, striving, living?" Throughout the Bible, people were led to change as God gave them hope.

## A REVIEW OF THE BIBLICAL IMPERATIVE

In chapter 3 we saw that Cain, though he had committed a brutal murder, was not allowed to waste his life; God gave him hope. In the account of Adam and Eve, God dared to gamble on humanity's choices only because he knew that, given hope, the experiment could be redeemed. David and dozens of other great Old Testament characters committed crimes against God, were punished by him, but always were given hope.

In the New Testament the Scriptures indict us all in crimes against God, but then we are given hope.

> Such a hope is no mockery, because God's love has flooded our inmost heart through the Holy Spirit he has given us. For at the very time when we were still powerless, then Christ died for the wicked (Romans 5:5-6, *New English Bible*).

In God's revelation of himself to sinful men and women, he always gives hope! Can Christians, then, remain idle while those with whom we share the same sinful nature are stripped of hope?

## THE DESTRUCTION OF HOPE

Ramsey Clark in his book, *Crime in America*, writes:

> If we are to deal meaningfully with crime, what must be seen is the dehumanizing effect on the individual of slums, racism, ignorance and violence, of corruption and impotence to fulfill rights, of poverty and unemployment and idleness, of generations of malnutrition, of congenital brain damage and prenatal neglect, of sickness and disease, of pollution, of decrepit, dirty, ugly, unsafe, overcrowded housing, of alcoholism and narcotics addiction, of avarice, anxiety, fear, hatred, hopelessness and injustice. These are the fountainheads of crime.[1]

These are not only the fountainheads of crime, but also they are the destroyers of hope. When these forces have finished their destructive work, they dump a man or a woman into prison like a machine that packages hopelessness.

Once society has done these kinds of things to a person, can prisons undo the damage? We have tried schemes to make this occur. One such scheme was the "indeterminate sentence"; i.e., a sentence whose length was initially not stated but which would be related to the inmate's behavior. The result was not to increase hope, but to decrease it.

> California has admitted that its 10-year experiment (1959–1969) in indeterminate sentences not only failed to reduce the number of repeaters but increased the median time served from two to three years. That state now requires a firm release date set after early review.[2]

The very word "indeterminate" implies hopelessness. Given an understanding of the importance of hope, it would not have been hard to predict the failure of such a scheme. One inmate could have instructed the reformers at this point: "As long as it has an end, it makes a big difference. When you can't see the end, it's forever."

In the rare cases where a person through his own inner resources finds hope within prison, it often cannot survive long in this environment. An inmate put it this way in a statement quoted in chapter 4:

> Everybody in jail reaches a point where he knows he doesn't want to go to jail again. But then the years pass, and he rots beyond that point until his hope turns to hate and you turn out a criminal.

How can prisons ever be expected to restore hope when, out of the $1.5 billion spent annually on "correction," 95 percent goes for custodial costs and only 5 percent for education, job training, health services, and other items associated with any kind of rehabilitative hope?[3]

Hope is still being destroyed in our prisons, and current rescue efforts are far too feeble for change. Prison and the record that goes with it, written on the mind and in the courts, is a modern mark of Cain. Only now it is not a mark of forgiveness and hope, but of ostracism, condemnation, and hopelessness.

## A CRY FOR HELP

All this is not happening without protest. Even with the crushing pressures of hopelessness, cries can be heard from within prison walls. At this writing, "Hurricane" Carter (top middle-weight boxing contender in 1966) is in the Rahway (New Jersey) State Prison. While he maintains his innocence, his cry for hope can be found on the lips of any prisoner who still has enough life to fight hopelessness. This quote is taken from a review of Carter's recent book, *The Sixteenth Round*, written by Frank Earl Andrews, another inmate.

> It's not only the story of one man, but of thousands who begin their education in reformatories and state homes. Most are not as strong as Rubin Carter; yet even he finds it necessary to ask for help in the end: "I come to you in the only manner left open to me. I've tried the courts, exhausted my life's earnings, tortured my two loved ones with little grains and tidbits of hope, that may never materialize. Now the only chance I have is in appealing directly to you, the people, and showing you the wrongs that have yet to be righted—the injustice that has been done to me. For the first time in my entire existence I'm saying that I need some help. Otherwise, there will be no more tomorrow for me, no more freedom, no more injustice, no more state prison, no more Mae Thelma, no more Theodora, no more Rubin, no more Carter. Only the 'Hurricane.'
> "And after him, there is no more."[4]

Rubin Carter speaks for many who are less articulate. Those who are guilty do not want to be declared innocent, but they do cry for hope. If this hopelessness could in some way help the innocent victims of their crimes, then there would be some justification for this destruction of hope. Since hopelessness helps no one, the cry for hope is justified; without it life has no meaning and prisons are for the living dead.

It is important to remember, as mentioned in chapter 6, that a sentence of life imprisonment is not required to kill hope. Hope is often killed within months. Within moments after the iron doors slam shut, hope begins to die.

> Imagine yourself, at age of eighteen or twenty, thrust into a society where forced homosexuality is an everyday occurrence, where murder and extortion are facts of life to be reckoned with as the "breaks" of the game, and where the aforementioned experiences are often viewed with tacit consent by the administrators of the society, since they keep the subjects in line.[5]

Yes, there is a cry for hope, but the cries do not last very long in that society. Eventually, even the spirit of a "Hurricane" Carter is crushed and ". . . there is no more." If the church does not listen soon and listen carefully, we will not hear the cry until it is too late—for prisoners and for us.

## THE RESTORATION OF HOPE

It is not completely fair to say that prisons destroy hope. Society has already largely destroyed hope in most of those who commit crimes; prisons simply finish the job. We create both the society and the prison. We are responsible—those of us who accept and do nothing about the kinds of conditions Ramsey Clark describes earlier in this chapter. Some may try to wash their hands of this responsibility; Christians cannot. It is our Lord who says, "I was in prison and you came to me" (Matthew 25:36). We must be the ones who go beyond existing systems to give hope. In an address to the Fellows of the Menninger School of Psychiatry, Paul E. Wilson said, "We forbid, we arrest, we coerce, we incarcerate, we parole, we treat . . . but we never forgive."[6] Christians uniquely know the hope that comes with forgiveness. They know both that they need forgiveness as much as anyone and that forgiveness has been offered in Christ. Therefore, the restoration of hope is a uniquely Christian responsibility. But how?

There are three fronts on which the Christians can act to restore hope. First, there are the kinds of prison ministries described in this book. These restore hope by offering redemptive change to the person, the prisoner. This approach is not a complete cure for hopelessness. Some would say that it is only tinkering with a demented machine and therefore ineffective. But we cannot wait until we solve the problems of society or until we have a better system of justice or until we find alternatives to prisons before we act to restore hope on this person-to-person basis.

Second, we can act to restore hope by reforming the penal system, including prisons. Churches like ours are discovering a similar experience to that of Christ Church, Presbyterian, in Burlington, Vermont.

> After several years of friendly visitation, the group agreed they could not be serious about prisoners without changing the county jail system.[7]

For those churches ready to move in this area, many of the groups listed in the Appendix also have an action program of penal reform. There is an active Prison Society in Pennsylvania[8] and in some other states. The National Council on Crime and Delinquency[9] is also active in prison reform. Many Christian denominations have developed their own task forces for penal reform; for example, The United Presbyterian Church, U.S.A., has a Task Force on Penal Reform that produced the document "Justice and the Imprisoned" for the 184th General Assembly,[10] and the American Baptist Churches of the U.S.A. has a Task Force on Criminal Justice and Prison Reform.[11] There are many places where a concerned church can act in the area of restoring hope to the system.

Third, we can act to restore hope by changing society. This takes us full circle, back to the local church and the leaven of its people in society. We all know that the ultimate solution to the problems of crime, prisons, and the penal system lies in a changed society, and that a changed society means changed people. This is what we say that the mission of the churches is all about. However, when we put it in these vast terms, the job of transforming society seems impossible. We often find ourselves seduced by despair, and we fail to do what we can do. We must resist this temptation and remember the power that was given to us for this task. "But you will receive power when the Holy Spirit comes upon you; and you will bear witness for me in Jerusalem, and all over Judaea and Samaria, and away to the ends of the earth" (Acts 1:8, *The New English Bible*).

A church that is being the church of Jesus Christ will act to restore hope by offering redemptive change to persons in prison, to the systems that process them, and to the society that creates them.

> I am but one, but I am one;
> I cannot do much, but I can do something;
> What I can, so I ought to do;
> And what I ought to do, by the Grace of God,
> I will do.
>
> Francis Willard

# The Way Others Have Traveled

In our own learning process we became aware of other churches and groups carrying on significant prison ministries. Because the need is so great and the possibilities for ministry so varied, five are included here that are especially significant and unique. They are: Yokefellows International, Norfolk Fellowship Foundation, M-2 Sponsors/Job Therapy, Scarsdale Congregational Church, and PACE Institute, Inc. These five meet the following criteria:

1. There is material available defining the purpose and methods of the program.
2. The program either was initiated by or received its major support from Christian churches or individuals in churches.
3. The program has a history of at least two years to demonstrate effectiveness.
4. The program offers insights that can be used by a local church or cluster of churches.

These criteria could include dozens of programs, but we have chosen those that show the wide variety of redemptive efforts that are possible. For each program selected the following information is listed:

1. A brief history
2. The stated purpose
3. Methods and activities
4. An evaluation

Evaluations are based on the relevance of the program for a local church, the clearness of biblical and theological foundations, and the effect of the program as seen by the participants. In some cases not enough information was available to evaluate fully all of these areas.

An additional word needs to be said about the lack of emphasis on programs relating to women in prison. This lack is due to the fact that 95 percent of all prisoners are men.[1] Many of the programs described can be and are effectively used with women in prison.[2] However, our experience and that of most of the programs described in this chapter is with men in prison.

## YOKEFELLOWS INTERNATIONAL
230 College Avenue
Richmond, IN 47374

### History

The idea of the Yokefellow Movement was conceived by Dr. D. Elton Trueblood, the well-known Quaker theologian and philosopher. It includes a prison ministry. The first Yokefellow-Spiritual Growth Group in a prison was formed in the U.S. Penitentiary at McNeal Island in 1955. It has since spread across the United States, and there are now about five hundred Yokefellow groups in prisons in every state. The title "Yokefellow" comes from Matthew 11:29, "Take my yoke upon you, and learn from me," and Philippians 4:3, "I ask you also, true yokefellow, help. . . ."

### Purpose

The following is the statement of purpose of the Yokefellow Prison Ministry:

1.  To help serve the religious needs of residents in correctional institutions. This is done through small spiritual growth groups which offer the inmate an opportunity to examine his life, and give him a chance to talk about his faith with others who also seek to discover a constructive direction and purpose for their lives.

2.  To bridge the gulf between persons confined and those of the outside community. In the relationships which evolve in small group discussions those persons who are confined begin to see that there are those from the outside community who do care and are willing to offer help. In order for the

confined person to reenter society successfully, the gulf between the confined life and the free life must be bridged. Association with persons from the outside community helps bridge that gulf.

3. To demonstrate a continuing concern for offenders in the process of reintegration into society. Reintegration into society is the primary function of rehabilitation of inmates. The Yokefellow Prison Ministry believes that our concern is a continuing concern, a concern that continues beyond the inmate's parole.

4. To encourage the establishment and operation of local community sponsored "halfway house" facilities. There is an established need for a network of residential facilities to assist convicted offenders who are returning to the free community upon being released from prison. Residential facilities not only provide housing for ex-offenders, but also can enable more of them to receive assistance in coping with the problems they face in making the transition between confinement and freedom. In some instances, halfway houses can serve as alternatives to prison for nonviolent offenders.

5. To minister to persons on probation and those confined to city and county jails, and to provide support and fellowship to those involved in services to such persons.

6. To initiate cooperative efforts to meet the needs of inmates and their families. The Yokefellow Prison Ministry seeks to meet the needs of inmates and their families by finding outside groups who through their resources can bring relief to the family or inmate. Such groups would include Cooperative Ministries and Urban Ministries.

7. To participate in programs designed to improve correctional methods including the exploration of alternatives to incarceration for nonviolent offenders.

## Method and Activities

Yokefellow meetings are extremely varied depending on the personality and needs of the leader(s) and participants. A quote from a brochure entitled "Greater Philadelphia Yokefellow Prison Ministry"[3] describes the methods I have observed in meeting with this group:

Yokefellow meetings are composed mainly of Bible-study and group therapy; dealing with how to relate with another "today," in our times. To do this, there must be honesty; real problems must be faced and answers found for real individual and group needs. Flexibility must be maintained to meet new and changing situations. Genuine love and concern must be shared so that healing may take place; this is "catharsis." Only then can individuals and groups practice "synthesis"—the practice of reaching out a helping hand to others. As all this takes place the Christian gospel becomes truly "good news" in action—and that is what it is all about.

These Yokefellow groups, although overtly Christian, are open to all interested persons. This same brochure of the Philadelphia group states:

The Yokefellow movement is for anyone who belongs to a Christian Church, anyone who is a Christian or is considering becoming a Christian, or anyone who is curious about the Christian faith.

Yokefellow also has a minimum discipline by which each member is to seek to live. This is also quoted in the same brochure from the Philadelphia group.

As one who seeks to wear Christ's yoke and learn from him, I accept with serious intention the following disciplines:
1. The Discipline of Prayer. To pray every day, preferably at the beginning of the day.
2. The Discipline of Scripture. To seek God's guidance through reverent reading of the Bible each day, following a definite plan.
3. The Discipline of Worship. To participate, at least once each week, in the public worship of God.
4. The Discipline of Money. To return to God a definite portion of my income to support the Christian cause.
5. The Discipline of Service. To allot a specific amount of my time in humble acts of love and service to others.
6. The Discipline of Witness. To make an unapologetic witness in daily life, daily work, and daily words.
7. The Discipline of Study. To become a better informed Christian by careful study of Christian books.

This discipline is not rigidly enforced in the prison work of Yokefellow, but it is a background ideal.

Yokefellow groups sometimes begin at the instigation of the prison chaplain, sometimes because of the interest of a local clergyman and, in one case I observed, at the insistence of an inmate. Upon transfer from another prison, this inmate pestered the chaplain until a group was established in his new setting.

Training for leaders (who often are laymen) is usually available, and published manuals to assist groups in theological and psychological skills are published by Yokefellow, available at the above address. Briefly, their method is one of small group dialogue in an atmosphere of honesty and acceptance.

## Evaluation

One of the reasons the Yokefellow ministry has endured and expanded is its flexibility. It allows each prison and each group to create its own emphasis. Since it insists on only the most basic framework of Christian belief and allows dissent on the part of the participants, it does not close itself off to the seeking doubter.

One ex-resident of federal prisons told me, "I saw five different Yokefellow groups; they varied from a very fundamentalist Bible study to a very open therapy group. The thing I found important was consistency and commitment." He also said, "Yokefellow was the only sane thing I saw in prison." Yokefellow also has groups for ex-inmates when they are released. Another inmate who was recently released told me, "It's hell in the street, especially if you're alone . . . once we get out, we try to help our Yokefellow."

Yokefellow's tendency toward a spiritual approach does not interest some inmates who have more militant and action-oriented needs. The principles of Yokefellow allow for and encourage action to remedy personal and institutional problems, but that action is not vigorous enough to suit some of the prison population. Yokefellow is used by a few inmates as a shelter from reality or a group with which to impress the parole board. This is an unavoidable risk in all prison religious groups.

In summary, Yokefellow has had a positive effect on those who participate, an effect which seems to last even "on the street." This is indicated by the statements of two ex-inmates who now participate in a Yokefellow group on the outside:

> It [Yokefellow] really got me together. I was just running all over the place.

> In the middle of the tensions and thrashing around, trying to make existence bearable, Yokefellow is a refuge and a place to stand . . . a place where we can get our heads together in preparation for action.

The Reverend David M. Myers, an institutional chaplain with

the United Methodist Church in Philadelphia, says, "In this cold world there are people who care because God cares for us . . . that is Yokefellow." This is the redemptive role Yokefellow seeks to supply.

## NORFOLK FELLOWSHIP FOUNDATION, INC.
### P.O. Box 331
### Mansfield, MA 02048

### History

The Norfolk Fellowship Foundation, Inc., began informally at the Massachusetts Correctional Institution at Norfolk, Massachusetts, as a fellowship group meeting on Sundays after Protestant services in 1957. The leadership was provided by the chaplain, Rev. Robert L. Dutton. The first step of growth was the inclusion of outsiders, called "outmates" in these groups. From this mix of inmate and outmate many social services and activities were established, such as suppers, speaking engagements for inmates, social education classes, establishment of a community worker for those newly released, small rap groups and a consciousness-raising program for area churches. The program is overseen by a Board of twelve officers and directors, two of whom are inmates. Their latest program is "Project Re-entry"[4] which allows ex-inmates to return to the prison to participate in the Fellowship's programs.

### Purpose

The following purpose was adopted by the Board of Directors, September, 1972, and is taken from the brochure entitled "Outline of the Correctional Services Offered by the Norfolk Fellowship Foundation, Inc."

> The Norfolk Fellowship Foundation, Inc. maintains a program in which people from the community enter into meaningful communication with inmates and former inmates of the Massachusetts Correctional Institution, Norfolk.
> The objective of the program is to create an atmosphere of fellowship, one that fosters mutual understanding, acceptance, and respect among its participants. The result is to enhance in each person a feeling of self-worth as part of the process of growth towards greater social maturity. It is expected that this program thereby contributes to meeting correctional objectives.[5]

**Method and Activities**

A brochure entitled "The Nature of the Fellowship" gives a good introduction to their method:

> The Fellowship can be described as a milieu in which people of varying backgrounds come together in mutual respect. The following characteristics suggest some of its dimensions.
> 1. The Fellowship exists partly at the institution and partly in the outside community. It offers continuity in relationships to inmates as they become ex-inmates and to any who return as inmates. The Fellowship endeavors to follow a man wherever he goes as long as he wishes it.
> 2. An attitude of caring for one another is seen in the fact that people from the outside take the time to meet with men for whom they have no individual personal responsibility. It is evident also in the friendliness in which inmates respond to outmates and in the warmth of the continuing relationships in the community.
> 3. The diversity of background among varying inmates and outmates provides one of the most valuable opportunities in the Fellowship experience.
> 4. Openness of expression of viewpoints by inmates has been often noted. Outmates are encouraged to speak their minds freely and as frankly as inmates.
> 5. While many members are keenly interested in prison reform, emphasis has been placed on concern for the individual now in the system so that he may be given maximum support both within the institution and on his release to the outside world.
> 6. While mindful of the practical needs such as employment or financial assistance the Fellowship has focused on the individual inmate or ex-inmate as a person on the assumption that if a human being can get his life together he will then be able to handle most practical matters himself.[6]

Present activities include a number of inmate-led groups with a few outmates participating in each and a more structured smaller group program called "social education" for the purpose of facilitating growth toward greater social maturity where the inmate to outmate ratio is usually two to one.

The outside program includes monthly meetings where former inmates and outmates can keep in fellowship and support. An annual conference is scheduled in the fall, and a picnic is held in the summer. A newsletter is also published. The Fellowship sees itself as a bridge over the walls. The newsletter of January 8, 1974, states:

When our program works well a man going out can have a corps of people who are his friends. He goes out of prison not friendless, or having to turn to men and women who were part of his earlier difficulties—he goes out with many close friends, who are in his corner. We see this often enough to keep us going, but we are also constantly saddened that this happy result comes to so few men.

The most recent activity is "Project Re-Entry" that allows selected ex-inmates to return to the prison to participate regularly in Fellowship activities. The rationale for this was:

> Inmates formerly heard only the negative aspects of life on the outside, saw only the failures. Now they see success. The Project has inspired many men to feel, "He made it. I can too!" It has also helped many inmates to a better understanding of the realities and frustrations they will face and to see some of the ways in which these can be overcome.[7]

Even though the Fellowship is nonsectarian, the base of operations of the Fellowship has been the area churches. Currently about twenty-five congregations are involved. Financial support and outmate participants have generally been supplied from these churches. While not overtly Christian, both in purpose and in spirit the Fellowship implements the Scripture on its brochure:

"... for I was in prison and you came to see me" Matthew 25:36

### Evaluation

The Norfolk Fellowship has made specific efforts at increasing an inmate's chances of making it on the outside. These visible efforts within prison walls have given it considerable credibility with inmates. In addition, because this group has prepared well for each new project, it has earned credibility with the prison administration as well. Earning this kind of credibility appears to be one of the most important ingredients in a prison ministry. Redemptive effects are definitely enhanced when a Christian group is able both to initiate and to follow through on effective programs. Personal contacts in groups and rap sessions allow follow-up (if appropriate) of an inmate's personal needs. The broad spectrum of programs sponsored by the Fellowship increases the probability that an inmate will see Christianity in more than its "spiritual" dimensions.

The Fellowship does seek a redemptive role and seems to succeed very well in the area of social and psychological relationships. However, the very broadness of its base of support can make it difficult for it to have a strong biblical thrust. To the extent that an inmate's problems may have a spiritual base in a broken relationship with God, the Fellowship's programs could miss his real need. This is the continuing dilemma of all church prison ministries: how to keep the spiritual, psychological, and social dimensions of redemption in balance—how to have a total ministry.

## M-2 SPONSORS, JOB THERAPY OF CALIFORNIA
Suite 213, 926 J. Street
Sacramento, CA 95814

### JOB THERAPY, INC.
2210 N. 45th St.
Seattle, WA 98103

### History

M-2 (which means match-two) grew out of the concern of Dick Simmons, a Presbyterian minister in Snohomish, Washington.[8] During his visit in the nearby Monroe State Reformatory he sensed the deep personal loneliness and hopelessness of the men there. He researched both the Scriptures and other prisoner rehabilitation programs before the M-2 idea was formulated. The program began with laymen from local churches visiting inmates at Monroe. It grew to reach other correctional institutions and expanded into a job placement and education program known as Job Therapy, Inc. The program begun in Washington State has been used as a model for other states, California having a very large M-2, with over six thousand sponsors.

### Purpose

The purpose of M-2 is to give an inmate or parolee a feeling of self-worth through the personal interest of his M-2 sponsor and the upgrading of skills and confidence through the program.

While there are no religious strings attached, the program has the further purpose of sharing the insights of Christianity, especially as this relates to the worth of each individual.

## Method and Activities

A typical procedure is described in the M-2 brochure for
California entitled, "M-2 Sponsors, Job Therapy of California."

> A citizen sponsor is matched with a prison inmate by Job Therapy
> of California. The program is voluntary on the part of both prisoner
> and sponsor.
> The sponsor visits his inmate friend at least once a month and
> corresponds with him. No special vocational or educational
> qualifications are required of the sponsor, but he should be the kind
> of person who will be a positive and wholesome influence. His
> relationship to the prisoner is that of a friend, not a counselor or
> teacher. Depending upon prison regulations the sponsor may also be
> able to involve his wife and children in the prison visits. Job Therapy
> orients new sponsors before the first visit and then stands by to help
> the sponsor when needed.
> When released, the sponsor continues to stand by the parolee as a
> friend.[9]

M-2 is well organized and, though it has deep Christian roots, is
funded through a number of secular agencies, for example, the
Federal Law Enforcement Assistance Administration. It makes its
main appeal for volunteers to the churches and has literature
describing how a church can become involved. The M-2 program
offers the following services to any church or group desiring to
begin the program:

1. Sponsor enlistment aids
2. Sponsor orientation
3. Matching services
4. Liaison with correctional officials
5. Bi-monthly newsletter
6. Evaluation
7. Reentry services

These services are without charge, but donations are accepted from
participating churches, groups, businesses, corporations, foundations, and individuals.

## Evaluation

M-2 is a unique combination of a strongly Christian motivation
and competent organization. It has won the admiration of prison
officials and inmates alike. Raymond Procunier, Director of
Corrections for the State of California, has said, "Community

corrections is the only way to go, and the M-2 program certainly has my support."[10] A personal letter sent to me from a former inmate not only stated that through M-2 "he found the Lord in prison," but also states that he went on to become an M-2 district representative.[11] A layman from the First Baptist Church of Pasadena wrote to tell me that he feels prisons are "the frontiers for mission" for any local church and has become a staff member of M-2 to implement that belief.[12]

There are interesting by-products when "straight people" enter prisons to maintain contact with an inmate. Warren Rawles, who was associated with a similar program in Texas, notes: "It is a fact of life that a prisoner who has visitors is treated better by the institution staff. If this well-dressed man starts showing up every Sunday to visit 70044, then the guards are going to say to themselves, 'I'd better be careful. I don't know what that inmate is going to tell that man.' And when they find out that man makes weekly reports to us, and we have a direct communication with the power structure, you better believe 70044 is going to get good treatment."[13]

The greatest problem with the M-2 program is the volunteer without staying power. While this plagues all types of volunteer programs, prisoners who have so few hopes to hang onto are more easily devastated when they feel volunteers or sponsors have let them down. M-2 is not unique in having this problem, but because of its personal man-to-man (or woman-to-woman) approach, it is more susceptible to this failing. A newsletter of the M-2 program in Hayward, California, notes the damage that can be done when a sponsor fails to show up or carry through:

1. Loss of trust an inmate has placed in you.
2. Disillusionment in another outside program.
3. Break of faith with M-2 staff, with state officials, and with institutional people.
4. Damage to your own integrity.

## SCARSDALE CONGREGATIONAL CHURCH
Dr. Roger W. Johnson
Scarsdale Congregational Church
1 Heathcote Road
Scarsdale, NY 10583

### History

In early 1971, Dr. Roger W. Johnson, pastor of the Scarsdale Congregational Church (twenty miles north of New York City), responded to a form letter inviting him to a conference on prisons and churches sponsored by the New York City Board of Corrections and Trinity Church on Wall Street. That experience combined with a growing awareness that he and his church were not living up to their calling to be agents of reconciliation led to the present prison ministries of this church. Dr. Johnson began by getting acquainted with inmates and administrators in order to find out what their needs really were. As his consciousness was raised, he shared this knowledge with the congregation by means of various speakers. A chaplain, a director of corrections, an inmate, and a musical group of ex-inmates all shared their insights with the congregation in that first year (1971). With this background the church has gradually and steadily reached out in a varied program of prison ministries.

### Purpose

The purpose of the prison ministries of this church is twofold. First—to minister to the alienated of society and to reach out to them as persons of value.

Second—to seek to change the criminal justice system in this country by becoming informed about the system and working for corrective legislation. The church believes present policies of crime control are self-defeating and that progressive change is in the self-interest of all of society.

### Methods and Activities

The church has a wide range of activities with a corresponding variety of methods. One of the first requests for ministry was from long-term inmates who requested letters, especially from females so that their world might have more normal contacts. This has been a continuing ministry of twelve to fifteen members of the congregation.

A more demanding congregational involvement has been through the "Threshold" program. This is a one-to-one program to develop problem-solving and decision-making skills among prisoners, developed by Dr. Milton Burglass.[14] It requires a three-day orientation program for volunteers. While this is not a church-sponsored program, volunteers from the church have found this an effective way to minister.

The church as a whole has sought to be an extended family for ex-inmates who have limited family contacts. This means sharing house, meals, and church activities with ex-inmates. They have also sought to upgrade library material in prisons where this has been requested and permitted. Other efforts have included support of a group known as "The Street Theatre, Inc." which provides an opportunity for dramatic expression by ex-inmates.

The church has joined with other area churches and synagogues to plan consciousness-raising workshops for the community with themes such as "After Attica—What?"

Dr. Johnson, himself, has continued his personal contacts with inmates and administration and has found it important to continue to share his insights through special presentations to the congregation by himself and by persons involved in every area of prison ministries.

Dr. Johnson also participated in the 42nd American Assembly, Columbia University, where contacts were made with criminologists, lawyers, and legislators. The results of this assembly have been edited and published under the title *Prisoners in America*.[15]

### Evaluation

In addition to the fact that this church has a significant program, it was selected for presentation here because it shows what a single local church can do under motivated leadership. The Scarsdale church is not atypical of suburban churches whose thoughts are traditionally far away from prisons. The following steps by the pastor made the difference between apathy and a significant ministry.

First, he had a sense of duty or a feeling of discontent over the prison and penal situation. Biblical imperatives were a factor in this sensitivity.

Second, he took the time to become informed through personal contact in the prisons and educational opportunities.

Third, he kept his congregation informed of his own growing understanding and permitted people related to prisons to create interest and concern among the members of his congregation. Because of this, the congregation has not opposed or hindered what some churches feel is an unattractive ministry.

Fourth, he let the congregation become personally involved. He recognized that no pastor can have an effective total ministry unless he allows and encourages his congregation to pick up the leads he has uncovered. They, in time, developed their own interest and momentum which multiplied any contribution he might have made acting alone. One of the reasons this pastor gave for his deep concern for this kind of redemptive ministry was that it exemplified the biblical theme of reconciliation for his church.

## PACE INSTITUTE, INC.
### 2600 S. California Avenue
### Chicago, IL 60608

### History

The history of PACE (Programmed Activities for Correctional Education) began with its founder, the Reverend John R. Erwin. At fourteen, John was told by a juvenile court judge, "I don't know how any boy could be as bad as they say you are, but I'm convinced you'll never adjust to life. I'm going to send you to a correctional institution and you'll probably spend most of your life in institutions."[16] John Erwin's life appeared to follow that prediction. Time in a supposedly "Christian" institution left strong negative impressions on him. Eventually Erwin was drafted during the Korean conflict. During this time he met Dave Pitman who showed Erwin a different kind of Christianity than Erwin had known previously, one of personal responsibility and concern. Erwin decided to give Christianity a try and even enrolled in a Bible school in order to become a missionary. During this time he had been assisting the chaplain at Cook County Jail, and when the chaplain left, the position was offered to Erwin. He has served the prison since that time. Erwin went through many changes in what he saw as the needs of the prisoners. The culmination of his insight was the establishment of PACE in 1967 for training prisoners in skills and attitudes that would help them make it on the outside.

Since that time PACE has grown into a major facility at the jail with a six figure budget funded by private contributions as well as government agencies. PACE still remains a privately run organization and relies heavily on volunteers.

## Purpose

PACE attempts to improve an inmate's self-image by upgrading his reading ability and vocational skills and by a social and spiritual ministry of committed volunteers.

## Method and Activities

Inland Steel Company of Chicago, Illinois, has shown an interest in the PACE program. In their company newspaper, *Inland Now,* they describe some of the program:

> There are . . . two criteria which a prisoner in Cook County Jail must meet to get into PACE: an expressed desire to change his lifestyle and at least four months remaining on his sentence. Once accepted, he is immediately moved to a special cellblock housing only PACE trainees. He takes a battery of tests to determine his strengths and weaknesses in basic education—the three Rs—and then starts schoolwork tailored to his individual needs, utilizing modern teaching machines with material developed specifically for PACE. He receives job instruction in any number of areas such as mechanics, carpentry, welding or draftsmanship. In the evenings volunteer tutors come to the jail to offer trainees individual instruction in areas ranging from creative writing to human relations.[17]

This evening program is staffed mainly by volunteers from churches who must be committed to a continuing and caring relationship with the PACE trainees. The Fourth Presbyterian Church of Chicago describes its involvement in the evening program in this way:

> The role of the Fourth Church volunteer, 25 of whom work in the program is a night-time one. Four nights each week, these dedicated men and women give, on a one-to-one basis, study assistance, friendliness, and guidance, and share their own life experiences— failures as well as successes—to provide for the inmate a much needed humane contact with "the outside." It is an intangible factor—a "tapping into" the lives of these volunteers which has proved in many instances to be the means of starting the participants on the road toward a useful and productive life after their release.[18]

Faith at Work and Moody Bible Institute also provide volunteers for this evening program which varies in style but in which openness is essential. Erwin insists that these groups allow the men to express their true feelings. One volunteer, Marty Pratt of Palatine Methodist Church, indicates something of this style when he says of his group, "You can't answer their questions by just quoting a verse from the Bible; you have to share the answers you're finding in your own life." [19]

## Evaluation

PACE works because John Erwin has the experience and commitment to make it work. It has the ingredients that help most in helping a person discover self-worth and the redemptive possibilities that go with this discovery. These ingredients are the upgrading of vocational and social skills and the personal concern of the evening volunteers.

The success of the program is reflected in the reduced rates of recidivism from 70 percent overall to less than 30 percent for PACE graduates. It might be argued that volunteers for such a program represent a select group that are already motivated to succeed. It is more likely that initially they are motivated by the better living conditions, social contacts, and the $20 per week stipend paid under a government contract. With love and concern PACE has been able to redirect these kinds of motives into more helpful and enduring ones. In the words of one trainee:

> There are two simple lessons that the sincere PACE trainee learns well. The first is that there is always room for the man of strength, for he makes his own room. A weak man cannot endure the burden of life. If he can receive and endure a wrong, if he can suffer and be silent, the man of strength sees a new possibility with the dawn of each day coming, and learns well the lessons of each day passing. The second is respect, based on accomplishments which can only be achieved by those who are humble, wise, and are themselves worthy of respect.
>
> I only regret that men must be subjected to the cruelty of confinement to become involved in a program that has the beauty of PACE.[20]

# Proposal of the Prison Committee, Royersford Baptist Church

Since 98 percent of all prisoners will be released to the community, most within five years, we, the prison committee, think it imperative that we, as a congregation, do all we can to insure as much as possible that the residents of Graterford be helped to succeed upon their return to society. To accomplish this, we recommend that the following proposals be adopted:

1. *Church support of rehabilitative activities*

   We propose that this congregation support the following programs:

   a. *Work Release*—Be on record as being in favor of this program. This program enables select residents who will soon be released to become accustomed to working in the community.

   b. *Discussion Groups at Prison*—Take part in these groups and/or support those who do. They help prompt much thought and personal growth both in the residents and visitors.

   c. *Outside Activities* (i.e., bowling, skating, etc.) by trusted inmates. These activities should be announced to the congregation and interested persons given the opportunity to take part in them.

2. *Individual support of rehabilitative activities*

   a. *Sponsorship of a Resident*—Sponsoring a Graterford resident is similar in some respects to what one does in sponsoring a refugee. Some of the residents have no positive contacts in the community and need to start afresh. Some have been in prison for so long that they do not know anyone on the outside. These men cannot be released unless they have a sponsor. Sponsors are supposed to give moral support and review the progress of the newly released resident. They are in no way legally responsible for him.

b. *Visiting and Writing*—There is a need for those who will visit or write residents within the prison who have no contact with friends or family outside the prison. The prison committee has the names of such individuals.

# NOTES

### Introduction

[1] The names of all inmates have been changed.

### Chapter 1

[1] These were of the type pioneered by the Church of the Saviour in Washington, D.C., and written about in Elizabeth O'Connor's *Call to Commitment* (New York: Harper & Row, Publishers, 1963).

[2] See Appendix A for information on the Yokefellow Prison Ministry.

[3] A copy of this resolution is in Appendix B.

### Chapter 2

[1] "Con," *The Random House College Dictionary,* rev. ed. (New York: Random House, Inc., 1975), p. 277.

[2] "Mark" and "Angela" are pseudonyms.

### Chapter 3

[1] L. Alexander Harper, "Prisons—Is There Any Hope?", *A.D. Magazine,* January, 1973, p. 36. Copyright *A.D.* Used by permission.

[2] Jackson wrote to his mother: "All my life now you have told me about European gods and European christians. . . . If there is a god, Mama, he hates me. . . ." *Soledad Brother, The Prison Letters of George Jackson* (New York: Coward-McCann, Inc., 1970), p. 88.

[3] In the Introduction to *Soledad Brother,* Jean Genet writes, "One might say that racism is here [in prison cells] in its pure state, gathering its forces, pulsing with power, ready to spring."

⁴Mimeographed statement from the Essex County Jail Task Force of the Presbytery of Newark, U.P.C., U.S.A., to the County Penal System Commission, Essex County, New Jersey, April 3, 1974.

⁵Karl Menninger, *The Crime of Punishment* (New York: The Viking Press, 1969), p. 153.

⁶Alan Paton, *Too Late the Phalarope* (New York: Charles Scribner's Sons, 1953), pp. 264-266.

⁷The United Presbyterian Church, U.S.A., 184th General Assembly (1972), *Justice and the Imprisoned* (Philadelphia: Board of Christian Education, U.P.C., U.S.A.), p. 33.

⁸Quoted in his book, *The Reconciling Gospel* (Valley Forge: Judson Press, 1960), p. 54.

## Chapter 4

¹Law Enforcement Assistance Aministration, "A Report on the Nation's Local Jails and Types of Inmates," *National Jail Census, 1970* (Washington, D.C.: U.S. Government Printing Office, 1971), pp. 2-4.

²*Corrections Magazine*, March, 1976, published by the American Bar Association, Commission on Correctional Facilities and Services, p. 10.

³Interview with Gary Smith, former inmate, on "Today" show, NBC, January 17, 1974.

⁴Chief Justice Warren E. Burger quoted in "Prisons—Is There Any Hope?", *A.D. Magazine*, January, 1973, p. 29.

⁵Patrick V. Murphy, "America Must Learn Correction Needs," *American Journal of Correction*, July-August, 1972, p. 22.

⁶Karl Menninger, *The Crime of Punishment* (New York: The Viking Press, Inc., 1968).

⁷Ramsey Clark, *Crime in America* (New York: Simon & Schuster, 1970), p. 225.

⁸The rate of recidivism is defined as the percentage of inmates who are returned to prison on an additional charge.
This quote is part of testimony given at the Citizens Hearings on Human Rights, Philadelphia, Pennsylvania, September 23, 1974, and quoted in a mimeographed letter from the Pennsylvania Prison Society (no date).

⁹Warden Adam McQuillan quoted in *A.D. Magazine*, January, 1973, p. 35.

¹⁰Raymond K. Procunier, Director, California Department of Corrections, quoted in *U.S. News and World Report*, December 16, 1974, p. 46.

¹¹Warden Adam McQuillan, *op. cit.*

¹²Quoted in *Liberty to the Captives* (Mennonite Central Committee Peace Section), vol. 3, no. 1 (March, 1974).

¹³David Janzen, editorial in *ibid.*

¹⁴Chaplain James McGee, "Penology," *Input* (American Baptist Churches), vol. 3, no. 39 (December 21, 1972).

[15] Chaplain Supervisor (unnamed), state of Maine, in a mimeographed article "A View of the Place of the Church in the Treatment of the Offender," October 6, 1971.

[16] Carl Hart, former director of religious services for the Tennessee Department of Corrections quoted in an interview by Walker Knight, "The Long Thin Line of Trust," *Home Missions* (Southern Baptist Convention), November, 1972, p. 23.

[17] Chaplain Charles R. Davis, Washington State Reformatory, Monroe, Washington, in a printed memo to other chaplains, n.d.

[18] Chaplain Supervisor (unnamed), state of Maine, in a mimeographed article, "A View of the Place of the Church in the Treatment of the Offender," October 6, 1971.

[19] Warren Rawles, U.S. Federal Reformatory, El Reno, Oklahoma, quoted in an interview by Everett Hullum, "The V.I.C. Freedom Caper," *Home Missions* (Southern Baptist Convention), November, 1972, p. 50.

[20] Gary Anderson, Chief of Chaplains for the State of Tennessee, quoted in an article by Jim Newton, "The Man Who Freed the Prisons," *Home Missions* (Southern Baptist Convention), November, 1972, p. 58.

[21] Chaplain Byron Eshelman quoted in *Liberty to the Captives* (Mennonite Central Committee Peace Section), vol. 3, no. 2, April, 1974.

[22] Edward Bunker, writing in *Harper's*, February, 1972, quoted in *Justice and the Imprisoned*, Statement and Background Paper, 184th General Assembly (1972) The United Presbyterian Church, U.S.A., p. 28.

[23] James Douglass, "Prison," from *". . . And the criminals with him . . ."* Luke 23:33, ed. Will D. Campbell and James Y. Holloway (New York: Paulist Press, 1972), p. 126.

[24] Eldridge Cleaver, *Soul on Ice* (New York: McGraw Hill Book Company, 1968), p. 5.

[25] Quoted by Raymond K. Procunier, *op. cit.*, p. 47.

[26] Quoted by Walden Howard, "A Quiet Center of Power," *Faith at Work Magazine*, February, 1974, p. 8.

### Chapter 5

[1] William Knight in a lecture on "Adolescent Behavior" at Princeton Theological Seminary, May 15, 1973, reported on a survey of inmates in the Mercer County, New Jersey, prison system. He quoted this survey as reporting that 95 percent of the inmates accepted the guilt for their crimes. This also has been our experience in prison.

[2] Michael Fedo, "Minnesota Felons Make Restitution," *The Sign*, November, 1973, pp. 33-34.

[3] Delaware Session Laws 1969, ch. 198, Pennsylvania Statute, paragraph 5109, added Laws of 1970, P.L. 257, cited in National Council on Crime and Delinquency, *Crime and Delinquency* (Continental Plaza, 411 Hackensack Ave., NJ 07601).

[4] For a brief account of the role of the Christian church in the early days of our prison system, see L. Alexander Harper, "Prisons, Is There Any Hope?" *A.D. Magazine*, January, 1973, pp. 28-36.

[5] While there is much doubt about the location of this text and some doubt about its authenticity, it is used here because I believe it accurately reflects the attitude of Jesus.

### Chapter 6

[1] See Erving Goffman, *Asylums* (Garden City, N.Y.: Anchor Books, 1961), for a description of the different world of the inmate, especially the idea of "disculturation," p. 13.

[2] See Thomas A. Harris, M.D., *I'm OK—You're OK* (New York: Harper & Row, Publishers, 1967), for a description of the four life positions (chapter 3).

[3] From an address to the Philadelphia Area Yokefellow groups at Graterford State Correctional Institution, Graterford, Pennsylvania, December 19, 1974. The kind of love needed is described in Bill Milliken's book, *Tough Love* (Old Tappan, N.J.: Fleming H. Revell Company, 1968).

### Chapter 7

[1] Karl Menninger, *The Crime of Punishment* (New York: The Viking Press, 1968); The United Presbyterian Church, U.S.A., *Justice and the Imprisoned* (Philadelphia: Council on Church and Society, 1972); George C. Kandle and H. Kris Ronnow, *The Fire in Today's Prisons* (New York: Office of Health and Welfare Strategy, United Presbyterian Church, U.S.A., 1972); Lawrence Baulch, *Return to the World* (Valley Forge: Judson Press, 1968); Will D. Campbell and James Y. Holloway, ed., ". . . And the criminals with him . . . , *Luke 23:33* (New York: Paulist Press, 1973).

[2] Robert J. Minton, Jr., ed., *Inside Prison American Style* (New York: Random House, Inc., 1971); Samuel Melville, *Letters from Attica* (New York: William Morrow & Company, Inc., 1972); George Jackson, *Soledad Brother: The Prison Letters of George Jackson* (New York: Coward-McCann, Inc., 1970); Erving Goffman, *Asylums* (Garden City, N.Y.: Anchor Books, 1970); George C. Kandle and Henry H. Cassler, *Ministering to Prisoners and Their Families* (Englewood Cliffs, N.J.: Prentice Hall, Inc., 1968); Jessica Mitford, *Kind and Usual Punishment: The Prison Business* (New York: Alfred A. Knopf, Inc., 1973).

[3] Fortune Society, *Fortune News*, 29 E. 22nd St., New York, NY 10010; Mennonite Central Committee, Peace Section, *Release*, 21 South 12th St., Akron, PA 17501; *VIP Examiner*, 200 Washington Square Plaza, Royal Oak, MI 48067; National Council on Crime and Delinquency, *Crime and Delinquency* (Continental Plaza, 411 Hackensack Ave., NJ 07601).

[4] Kandle and Ronnow, *op. cit.*

[5] See Thomas A. Harris, M.D., *I'm OK—You're OK, A Practical Guide to Transactional Analysis* (New York: Harper & Row, Publishers, 1969).

### Chapter 8

[1] Ramsey Clark, *Crime in America* (New York: Simon and Schuster, 1970), p. 17.

[2] L. Alexander Harper, "Prisons, Is There Any Hope?" *A.D. Magazine*, January, 1973, p. 31.

[3] Clark, *op. cit.*, p. 213.

[4] Frank Earl Andrews, "Will 'Hurricane' Carter Win His Biggest Fight?" *The Sunday Bulletin* (Philadelphia) November 17, 1974.

[5] Robert J. Minton, Jr., ed., *Inside Prison American Style* (New York: Random House, Inc., 1971), p. xv.

[6] Karl Menninger, M.D., *Whatever Became of Sin?* (New York: Hawthorne Books, Inc., 1973), pp. 51-52.

[7] Harper, *op. cit.*, p. 34.

[8] The Prison Society of Pennsylvania, Social Service Building, 311 South Juniper Street, Philadelphia, PA 19107.

[9] National Council on Crime and Delinquency, Continental Plaza, 411 Hackensack Ave., Hackensack, NJ 07601.

[10] Available from: General Division of Church Educational Services, Board of Christian Education, The United Presbyterian Church, U.S.A., Room 1115, Witherspoon Building, Philadelphia, PA 19107.

[11] Information available from: Task Force on Criminal Justice and Penal Reform, Rev. Paul Strickland, American Baptist Churches, U.S.A., Valley Forge, PA 19481.

## APPENDIX A

[1] U.S. Bureau of the Census, *Survey of Inmates of Local Jails*, 1972.

[2] A Yokefellow program was begun in our area at the State Correctional Institution for women at Muncy, Pennsylvania, under the direction of Chaplain Muriel Parker.

[3] Mimeographed brochure available from:
Greater Philadelphia Yokefellow Prison Ministry
c/o The Reverend David M. Myers
3530 Carey Road
Philadelphia, Pennsylvania

[4] Marie Buckley, "Enter the Ex-Con," *Federal Probation*, March, 1973.

[5] Mimeographed brochure available from:
Norfolk Fellowship Foundation, Inc.
Box 43
Norfolk, MA 02056

[6] *Ibid.*

[7] Norfolk Fellowship Foundation, *Project Re-Entry*, Brochure, n.d.

[8] Bonnie Greene, "These Christians Show the Way," *Eternity*, September, 1973, p. 16.

[9] Printed brochure available from:
M-2 Sponsors, Job Therapy of California
Suite 213, 926 J. Street
Sacramento, CA 95814

10 Raymond K. Procunier, "Why Prisons Fail," *U. S. News & World Report*, Dec. 16, 1974.

11 Personal letter from Jerry Graham, M-2 District Representative, May 8, 1974.

12 Personal letter from Edwin Phelps, Jr., M-2 District Representative, June 25, 1974.

13 Everett Hullum, "The V.I.C. Freedom Caper," *Home Mission Magazine* (Southern Baptist Convention), November, 1972, p. 50.

14 For more information write Milton E. Burglass, M.D., Correctional Solutions, Inc., 22 Ellsworth Avenue, Cambridge, MA 02139. Dr. Burglass is an ex-inmate.

15 Lloyd E. Ohlin, ed., *Prisoners in America* (Englewood Cliffs, N.J.: Prentice-Hall, Inc., 1973).

16 Walden Howard, "A Quiet Center of Power," *Faith at Work Magazine*, February, 1974, p. 7.

17 "No Bars to Learning," *Inland Now*, n.d.

18 "PACE . . . An Opportunity to Show You Care," *4th Focus*, Fourth Presbyterian Church, Chicago, Illinois, n.d.

19 Howard, *op. cit.*, p. 8.

20 "PACE Trainee Tells It Like It Is," *PACE Institute News*, Programmed Activities for Correctioal Education, Chicago, Illinois, May, 1973.